2 cop.
ea 4.00

D1063923

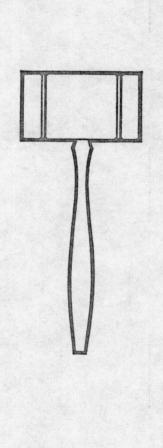

THE
MURDER
TRIAL
OF
JUDGE
PEEL
BY
JIM
BISHOP

A TRIDENT PRESS BOOK   Simon and Schuster, New York

Dedicated to
William Randolph Hearst, Jr.,
who found this story
first.

CONTENTS

Part Two: The Trial (*Continued*)

FOR THE
RECORD:

Murder is a fairly common concomitant of civilization. One of the weaknesses of the coat of varnish we call culture is that it tends to crack. When it does, man becomes disorderly and violates the social rules in any number of ways—murder, if he's a citizen of a nation; a declaration of war, if he heads the nation.

The greatest murderer of all time is, of course, Adolf Hitler who, when he decided to send three German Armies into Poland in the cool autumn of 1939, became responsible for the 30,000,000 persons who in time died as a result of his action. The least of the murderers is the elderly man who, in a New Jersey bungalow, sat holding his sick wife's hand as she writhed in the agonies of cancer, and when he could bear it no longer, killed her, wept over her, and walked bareheaded to the nearest police station.

Between these are the killers for profit, for passion, for fear, for revenge, for freedom, for love, for a variety of reasons from the trivial to the enormous and compulsive. As a writer I have sometimes chronicled the trials of the big murders, and of them all I consider this the weirdest and most complex.

A charming and respected municipal judge of Palm Beach—Joseph A. Peel—was charged with the murder of a superior court judge, C. E. Chillingworth. Peel not only denied the crime, he was outraged by the charge. On the day that the jury deliberated his innocence or guilt, he and I sat at breakfast in the St. Lucie County Jail.

I asked him what would happen. He was a handsome charmer, and when he smiled the whole detention pen lit up. "It's going to be a hung jury," he said. I felt that he was wrong. I said so.

He asked what I thought would happen. I shrugged. There was no point in saying: "Under the rules of evidence, I think that they will come in with a verdict of guilty with no recommendation of mercy."

Matters were difficult enough for Peel without adding my amateurish prophecies to his problems. Still, what happened was, to my way of thinking, a shock.

To preserve the storyteller's art, I will not tell you now. However, I suggest that if you fancy yourself a reasonable human, one equipped to judge innocence and guilt, the complexity of this case will keep you engrossed. The cast of characters—ranging from the spitting contempt of Prosecutor Phil O'Connell for his one-time friend, Judge Peel, to the venom of the professional killer, Floyd Holzapfel, on the witness stand—could have come out of a motion picture.

The role of the witness neither side desired to call—Mrs. Floyd Holzapfel—will, I suppose, remain a mystery. It was said in court that the lady met Judge Peel in New York for a weekend to discuss the case. If this is so, and there is no reason to doubt it, then why did Mr. Holzapfel bristle and roar with rage every time her name was mentioned in conjunction with Judge Peel? And why did another witness, P. O. Wilber, claim that he planted a seed of jealousy in Holzapfel's mind?

I do not know. There is much that I do not know about this case. However, every facet of it that is a part of the public record is here for your perusal. And your judgment. Think carefully, and tell me your verdict.

Jim Bishop
Sea Bright, New Jersey

PART ONE

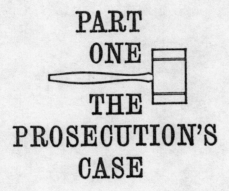

THE PROSECUTION'S CASE

There was a morning heat mirage on Route A1A. It was a little lake that wasn't there and it hung about 300 yards ahead of the car. The driver and his partner moved south, not talking much and not seeing much except the white line in the road and the mirage.

There was a beauty and elegance all around them. They passed the gorgeous beach mansions of the Wrightsmans, the Phippses, the Kennedys, the Hales, and their eyes reflected the neatly trimmed hibiscus, the poinsettia, the lawns like big blue rugs, the flaming orange orchids and the stately palm trees, but they saw them not.

Frank Ebersold and Robert Force were carpenters. They were

due at Judge Curtis Chillingworth's beach house to repair a window frame. Judge Chillingworth was a meticulous, humorless man. In the circuit court at West Palm Beach he used to stand outside the door at 9:29 A.M. studying his watch, the charge case in his other hand, waiting for the stroke of 9:30 to step into court and rap for order. He looked like a crane in rimless glasses.

The judge lived by the clock and the law books. Some say he had exactly seven friends.

Ebersold passed through Palm Beach and came to the super-exclusive little community of Manalapan. It had twenty-seven registered voters. The car turned left, toward the sea, into a small gravel drive. Dead ahead was a two-car garage. One car was in it.

Ebersold and his partner took their toolboxes and walked up the back stairway to the beach house. They knew their place and they knew the people. The judge had a town house at 211 Dyer Road, and in the wintertime he rented this beach house for a fat sum. Now it was summer—June 15, 1955—and Palm Beach was back down to its 2,500 permanent residents, and West Palm Beach, across Lake Worth, had 60,000 people.

The beach house had a flat roof and an open breezeway in the middle. It sat high on the sand dunes, facing the Atlantic. There was a rickety, one-banister stairway down to the beach. The house was done in gray deck paint and hanging from the porch was a ship's bell with a rope on the clapper. This was a memento of the days when the judge had been a navy commander stationed in Jacksonville.

The carpenters knocked. There was no doorbell. They could look through the glass jalousie of the door and see the small living room with its beige straw rug, the little bridge table for

4

breakfast, and the blue china dishes on the wall. There was a modern kitchen, and a nine by twelve bedroom in this wing. Here there were a night table, twin beds and a cream-colored phone. They knocked again. No answer.

There must be someone around, they figured, because Chillingworth's car was in the garage. They turned toward the other wing and stepped on broken glass. It came from an overhead spotlight on the porch. The light had been broken.

The second wing had two bedrooms with twin beds, plain dressers, and small lavatories. The doors were unlocked and no one was inside.

"Let's go for a swim," Ebersold said. The other man shrugged. They walked down the front steps of the house. The sea was as flat as a million tons of lime Jello. They walked across the pocked macadam of an old road and down the rickety steps.

"Look," said Force. His partner looked. There were stains on the steps. The carpenters bent and studied the dry drops. It was either paint or blood. They followed the stains down onto the beach. There were footprints in the sand, a lot of footprints. Some seemed to be from shoes coming out of the sea toward the house, others were heading back to sea.

The soft foamy waves of the morning tide were erasing the footprints as the men studied them. "I'm going to phone the judge's office," Ebersold said. He went back, got into his car, and drove to the nearest public phone. He told the judge's secretary that maybe nothing was wrong and maybe something was, but it didn't look right to him.

The secretary called the office of Sheriff John Kirk. In an hour, police officers were all over the house. Kirk, a veteran and a bulldog among sheriffs, crouched in a little thatched hut down on the beach, correlating everything his deputies found.

What they found was nothing more than what the carpenters had seen. There was no sign of a struggle inside the house. The stains were human blood. The footprints—who knows? The car was cold in the garage. The judge was overdue in court and Chillingworth had never been late.

The Chillingworth daughters were called. There were three—Ann (Mrs. George Wright); Marie (Mrs. William M. Cooper); and Miss Neva Chillingworth. They offered little. Mother and Daddy had been at their own town house last night, and had left for the beach house around dark—9 P.M. They were not in the house at Dyer Avenue, and the only evidence that they had been in the beach house was the rumpled beds, and two empty glasses which had held nightcap drinks.

The afternoon newspapers said that Judge Curtis Chillingworth and his wife, Marjorie, were missing under mysterious circumstances. Judge Chillingworth was the senior judge in the Fifteenth Judicial District of Florida and had been on the bench thirty-four years. He had served Florida with honor—yes, distinction. His father had been a lawyer, and up around Jupiter and Hobe Sound, the people had called him "judge."

That evening a laboratory technician established that the blood on the beach steps was human, of the same type as Mrs. Chillingworth's. Who would kill the Chillingworths? If they had few friends, then it was equally true that they had fewer enemies.

Judge Joseph A. Peel was the one and only municipal judge of West Palm Beach. He was the glamour boy of the legal fraternity, the handsome, wavy-haired, big-eyed epitome of the southern gentleman. He wore white linen suits and big horn-rimmed sunglasses. His salary wasn't much more than $3,000 a year and his clients were mostly poor Negroes and poorer whites, but he drove around in an air-conditioned Cadillac and his wife used a Lincoln Continental.

Judge Peel? He was born in West Palm Beach. His father was the owner of a small hotel; Buck Peel was popular. Everybody knew the Peels. Joe was only thirty-one, and he was already serving his second term as a judge. His office was in the Harvey Building at the corner of Olive and Datura, and the only gossip tied to his name was a sniveling report that the judge had a penchant for posing ladies nude next to his diploma on the wall, and then rushing the negatives off to the police laboratory for development and printing.

People always gossip over successful men. Judge Peel had begun the practice of law only in 1949 and now, six years later, he was the sole trier of all small cases in and around Palm Beach. His wife was the ladylike Imogene Clark of Lake City, Florida. They had two children and a big happy life in front of them.

The man who became most interested in the mystery also practiced law in the Harvey Building. He was Phillip D. O'Connell, the state attorney. Mr. O'Connell was a prominent Catholic layman, a prosecutor who had turned down better jobs, a lawyer who took in $100,000 a year in fees, a one-time professional welterweight fighter who had a record of fifty-nine wins in sixty fights.

Mr. O'Connell never thought much of Judge Peel. Once when Peel asked for a job, O'Connell said: "I have no job for you, Joe, but I have two vacant offices on the eighth floor. They're yours if you want them." Peel had accepted, and had put his name in gold letters on the door. Still, they were not friends. Nor enemies.

The more O'Connell thought of Peel, the less he thought of

7

him. It occurred to the prosecutor that Peel could have killed Judge Chillingworth. Still, he had no case. The Chillingworths were missing, not dead. And even if they were dead, there was nothing in any of the evidence to point to Peel. And yet—and yet O'Connell decided that perhaps he had better go back over the record of Judge Peel. He wanted to see where it crossed the life of Judge Chillingworth. He had a recollection of trouble between these men.

He was still working on it two years later when the courts of Florida declared Judge and Mrs. Chillingworth to be legally dead. Neither one has been seen since.

There is wealth here in Palm Beach. And poverty. The wealth is on a strip of sand along the ocean where a millionaire spends more on his flower gardens than a mechanic earns in West Palm Beach in a year. West Palm Beach is on the opposite side of Lake Worth, where the big yachts sit all winter, awaiting the pleasure of their owners.

Floyd Holzapfel was a mechanic in West Palm Beach. He was also a crook. He worked on cars by day and on people at night. Mr. Holzapfel had hair that waved back off a receding forehead. His face looked slept in.

The one thing that Holzapfel had on his side was nerve. When he found it necessary to fire a gun into the back of a man's head, he did not hesitate. If it was a duty to take a tiny woman and drop her into the sea at night, Holzapfel sat on his conscience and did it.

One day in 1953 he had a small claims court action. Someone advised him to try a good lawyer. Floyd went to see Municipal Judge Joseph A. Peel. These two conferred, and in no time at all the judge was calling Mr. Holzapfel by his nickname: Lucky. They got along.

The judge surprised Lucky by reciting some of the Holzapfel background. He said that Floyd had been a bookmaker in California when he was only seventeen years old. Lucky was impressed. The judge also knew that Holzapfel had been convicted, and pardoned, for two armed robberies in Florida.

It is ironic that such knowledge could be the basis for an enduring friendship. The mutual esteem grew, in time, to a partnership. It was such a happy situation that there was room for a third man. He was George David Lincoln, known to his friends as Bobby. Lincoln was a big Negro with a steady, mean stare. He asked few favors and granted none, even among his own people.

Lincoln was a power among the Negroes north of West Palm Beach. He had two poolrooms and two taxicabs and still worked a little job on the side. In addition, Bobby Lincoln was in the moonshine and bolita rackets in Palm Beach, but when he sat behind the wheel of his decrepit truck, he looked deceptively like a poor colored man trying to earn a desperate dollar.

Bobby could lend thousands of dollars, if he chose. In Holzapfel's case, he chose. According to Lincoln, he and Lucky and Judge Peel became partners in the sale of racket protection. The judge wanted $7 a week from everybody in the bolita racket and moonshine. Lucky supports Lincoln's contention in saying the judge got it.

The bolita racket is the old numbers game with a Spanish twist. The poor play any number from one to a hundred. They play any amount they please. If they have the right number, they are paid odds of seventy to one. The bolita operators keep the rest. About $10,000 a week is played in bolita in and around the Palm Beaches.

The cream comes to about $3,000 a week. The numbers runners get $1,000 of this, and that leaves $2,000. The operators of bolita were not satisfied with $2,000. They had to figure a way of fixing the game.

The winning number is determined by putting tiny plastic balls, with numbers on them, into a beanbag. It is tossed around in a group, and when the head racketeer yells "Stop," the person holding the bag reaches in and picks a ball. That's the winner.

The racketeers began to look over the daily lists of numbers played and decided it would be nice if the number played the least could be the winner. Let us say that very few people played number 17. The racketeers could fix the game in one of several ways: (1) have all the plastic balls in the beanbag, unknown to those who were throwing the bag around, numbered 17; (2) put plastic ball number 17 in a refrigerator, freeze it, and have a confederate pick the winning number merely by feeling inside the bag for one cold ball; (3) have a little pocket in the beanbag with the winning ball in it.

Holzapfel was in it. So was Lincoln. So, they claim, was Judge Peel. He also received money, his old friends say, from shine.

Shine (the word is a contraction of the word moonshine) is probably the oldest racket in Florida. The sale of moonshine is illegal. Tax-dodging liquor is distilled in all parts of the state. It is sold in jugs and Mason jars by the half gallon and gallon for a fraction of what legal liquor costs.

There is a third racket, smaller economically than the others, called Loteria Cubana. This one is based on a legal lottery manipulated in Cuba. The numbers selling in Cuba are duplicated in Florida by the racketeers, and they pay off on whatever number is drawn in Havana.

The state charges that Judge Peel took a little from everyone. If true, it was done with benevolence because when the police wanted to raid a bolita parlor or a shine saloon, they got their search warrants from Judge Peel. If he was crooked, he had three choices: (1) to make out the warrant and then warn the place in advance of the raid; (2) to draw up a defective warrant so that, when the bolita and shine racketeers were convicted, they would, on appeal, be acquitted; (3) to convict a few friends who were paying, and then deduct the small fine from the $7 a week they paid him.

Whatever the gallant judge was doing, he was doing it well when the roof fell in. On July 6, 1953, he was charged with representing both parties in a divorce action. The matter was heard by a judge of the Florida Circuit Court and referred for action to Judge Curtis Chillingworth.

Judge Peel was unhappy. He knew that Chillingworth was about as warm and friendly as a starving polar bear. The old judge was sudden death to shysters. Joe Peel worried himself sick waiting for the blow to fall. However, Chillingworth surprised the young man. He heard the evidence and he said that a public reprimand would suffice, "because of the youth and inexperience of counsel."

It was after this close brush that Judge Peel asked State Attorney Phil O'Connell if he wanted a lawyer to do some of his work. O'Connell declined and gave Peel office space until he could work up a practice. There is coldness in this, and warmth too. They shared O'Connell's reception room for a while, and the relationship was that of an older, successful man trying to give a youngster a break.

The next year—1954—Joe Peel ran for re-election as municipal judge, and won. His ambitions began to soar. He began to talk of the job of county solicitor, then state senator, and who knows?—the Governor's mansion in Tallahassee. Ambition is a mean master. It holds power in one hand and money in the other and seldom gives both and often gives neither.

Judge Peel was not a stupid man. He was bright and optimistic. It would appear, however, that he wanted to play both sides of the game and play them well. He wanted to gamble, and deal. Other Florida politicians shake down the racketeers—why not a young judge?

In the spring of 1955 he was in trouble again. He told a woman named Shupe that she was divorced when, in fact, she was not. Mrs. Shupe remarried and had a baby. Later, she and her new husband decided to adopt another baby. The adoption authorities checked her divorce decree and told her there was no record of it. Mrs. Shupe was an unconscious bigamist. She complained loudly.

The case against Judge Joseph Peel came before Circuit Court Judge Joseph White. The procedure in Florida is for such a matter to come before one superior judge and if he finds that there is cause for action, he refers it to another circuit judge.

In Palm Beach County there were only two: White and Chillingworth. The case reached the newspapers and Judge Chillingworth read about it. Judge Peel heard that Chillingworth had said that, this time, if Peel came before him for disciplinary action, Peel would never practice law in Florida again. Chillingworth would break Peel.

If this is true, the panic which beset Peel is understandable. He was badly frightened. Disbarment would mean loss of practice, loss of income, loss of prestige, loss of judgeship—the end of a career at the age of thirty-one. Peel's lawyer, John A. Paul, appeared before Judge White on or about June 1, 1955, and asked for a continuance until his client could locate his former secretary somewhere in Georgia.

White agreed to it. He said he would give Peel until June 15. At 9:30 A.M. on June 3, according to Floyd Holzapfel,

Joe Peel called Lucky in and said: "Judge Chillingworth is going to ruin me. The fact is he personally is going to take care of me when the case comes up." He stared at Lucky. "We'll have to get rid of the judge," he said.

The partnership in rackets between Peel and Holzapfel and Bobby Lincoln ran as high as $3,000 a week in shakedown money. Without Peel as a judge, Floyd and Bobby were out of business.

Floyd says he suggested Bobby Lincoln as an assistant. Peel said he could do nothing to help. On the fifth of June, 1955, Peel and Holzapfel drove up Center Street in Riviera Beach to the Lincoln home. They took Bobby in the car to Singer Island and parked on a dirt road.

"Bobby," Peel said, "a man is trying to ruin us and I have got to kill him."

Lincoln claims he asked: "What's he trying to do?" and the judge said: "Well, he is going to ruin everything that we have worked for and everything that we are doing."

The two white men began to discuss how to commit the crime, and Lincoln says they came up with an idea of kidnaping the judge, taking him off somewhere, and killing him. In that way it would look like a disappearance. Peel said: "Chillingworth doesn't move around much. The judge works on prompt time. He does everything in a pattern." The three agreed on a kidnaping-murder, and Floyd said that Judge Peel would have to point Chillingworth out; he didn't know what the man looked like.

Twice the judge took Lucky out in his car and pointed to a tall skinny man in spectacles. Twice Floyd studied the lean, limber gait and thought of how short a time this stranger had to live.

13

Lucky remembered that Joe Peel said it would be wise to get a boat, kidnap Judge Chillingworth from his summer house on the beach at Manalapan, take him out to sea and drown him. There would be no body, no corpus delicti, no witnesses, no clues, no case. How could anyone charge murder unless murder could be proved? It would be laughed out of court. In New York, Judge Crater disappeared many years ago and no one knows what happened to him. This would apply to Chillingworth if he were kidnaped at gun point, taken out to sea, properly weighted, and dropped over the side. There would be some publicity, of course. But nothing legal. The man had vanished, and might turn up any time. Any year.

The second week of June, 1955, was hot. Judge Curtis Chillingworth sat in court with his jacket on and looked down at counsel.

"As long as the public is not present at this hearing," he said, looking over the tops of his spectacles, "and as long as there are no witnesses present, I will listen to the argument of counsel without the discomfort of coats. You may take them off, gentlemen."

Chillingworth kept his on. He may have thought of how much cooler it would be to be sitting on his "bridge," the front porch of his beach house. He may have, but the chances are he did not. His love was the law and he equated everything, even casual household problems, according to the letter of the law.

But, whether Chillingworth did or not, Judge Joseph Peel might have been thinking of that beach house, for according to statements made by Lucky and Bobby, he drove to it, paused in the driveway, explained the rooms of the house to Floyd Holzapfel and Bobby Lincoln, and one evening when the house was empty and dark, he parked the car and waited while Floyd

14

walked through the brush to the beach side of the place to examine it. "When I do this thing," Lucky said, "I will call you at home. I'll just say: 'The motor's fixed.' Okay?"

Okay. On June 12 Lucky drove Lincoln to the Blue Heron dock and took him out on a little cabin cruiser. Both men liked to go spear fishing and both had the spears, the masks, the big cartridge-type belts and the lead weights to put in the belts. They went out by way of the Riviera Beach Inlet into the Atlantic Ocean.

They did no fishing. Bobby asked why they were out at sea. "There's good spear fishing on a reef out here," Lucky said. "Besides, I'm thinking of buying a boat like this."

Two evenings later, according to Lucky's confession, Peel told Lucky that the judge would be at his beach house that night. Mrs. Chillingworth wouldn't be there. It was her night to visit one of her daughters. Still, he said, Lucky and Bobby should go prepared. If there was a witness, Peel said, that person must be "destroyed because, if anyone makes one little mistake it will lead directly to the electric chair." He didn't have to add: "for all of us."

It was June 14, 1955, and Lincoln got home about 8:45 P.M. There was a little daylight left and he saw Holzapfel parked in his back yard. Bobby reached into the glove compartment of his car and put a revolver in his belt. He got into Floyd's car and they drove up Blue Heron Boulevard to the Riviera Beach dock. They got out and Floyd picked up a heavy croker sack from the floor behind the front seat. He slung it over his shoulder.

A yachting cap sat jauntily on Holzapfel's head. Lincoln asked him what it was for. Lucky said that Joe Peel had suggested that when they knocked on the Chillingworth door, it

15

would look good if they said they were from a sinking yacht. They would say they wanted to use the phone to call the Coast Guard.

It sounded logical. They got into the boat and Floyd got out again and came back with a bottle of whisky in a paper bag. It was dark now, and as they pulled out through the inlet, the moon was up over the sea. Lucky remained forward, at the wheel. He kept pulling at the bottle and handing it back to Bobby. The little boat headed east, then south, a mile and a half offshore, and the lights of Palm Beach came up bright on the starboard bow.

The engine heat indicator kept rising, and Floyd hit it with his hand, but it wasn't stuck. The engine was overheated. He stopped it, drifted a while, then started it again. They did this every fifteen or twenty minutes. Behind the boat, the propeller churned the phosphorescence of the sea, and millions of little lights winked on and off like flirtatious amoebae.

The bow wave picked up the broken pieces of silver from the moon and curled them back into the sea. There was no chill, and Lucky was in no hurry. It required an hour from the inlet to pass the Chillingworth house. A spotlight on a porch rafter pointed down to the beach.

"That's the house," Lucky said.

The little boat moved south of it, stopped a while, started again, stopped, turned back, passed the house, and then, after 1 A.M., turned and came in to the shore. Floyd turned the engine down and came in on the little swells. The moon had passed the zenith and it threw the shadow of the house onto the beach. He ordered Bobby to throw an anchor behind the boat, to seaward, so that the breakers could not hurl it up onto the beach.

The bow grated on sand, lifted, and grated again. Lucky left

16

the engine in low. This is a mistake in shallow water, because the engine sucks in clear water, preferably without sand, to keep it cool. He picked up the heavy croker sack and jumped out into a few feet of water. Bobby came out after him, and the boat rose and floated in another few feet.

They walked up the beach, up the rickety little stairway, and when they reached the steps of the porch, Lucky said, "You stay here. I will call you if I need you."

Bobby Lincoln crouched low in the bushes to the left of the stairway. Lucky fixed his cap, patted the gun under his sports shirt, and went up the stairs into the brazen light on the porch. He set the croker sack down, and since there was no bell, knocked on the living-room door.

There was no answer. He knocked again. A light switched on in the living room. A tall, thin man in pajamas opened the door. He was adjusting his glasses.

Holzapfel had a latent fear that he could be at the wrong house so he looked at the man, expressed pleasant surprise, and said, "Aren't you Judge Chillingworth?"

The judge nodded curtly. "I am."

Floyd said he was the captain of a sinking yacht and could he please use the phone to call the Coast Guard. The judge was framing an answer when Lucky reached under his shirt and pulled a gun out of his belt. "This," he said, "is a holdup. Is anyone else in the house?"

The judge looked at the gun, looked at the man, and said, "Yes."

Holzapfel waved the gun and said, "Then call them out."

The judge called, "Margie!" In a moment Mrs. Chillingworth, a small woman with dark hair and eyes, came out of the bedroom pulling a robe on over her nightgown.

Floyd whistled for Bobby Lincoln. "Knock that light out," he said. Lincoln reversed his gun and hit the porch light with the butt. The light died suddenly.

"Look in the house," Floyd said, "and see if anybody else is in there." Bobby moved in cautiously. The judge watched, and blinked. His wife stood a little behind him.

Lincoln looked around and came back. "I don't see nobody," he said. He was nervous. "What are you going to do with these people, Floyd?" He knew.

Floyd handed his gun to Bobby. "I am going to take them and put them on the boat," he said. "We are going to have to send them off for a few days. These are the people trying to mess up Joe."

Judge Chillingworth said nothing. If the name "Joe" meant anything to him, he kept his peace. He had another hour of life in which to dwell upon this solitary clue. If he knew that Joe meant Judge Peel, he didn't mention it. His attention was fixed on the Negro.

Floyd got some stuff out of the croker sack. He put a light-line noose around the judge's neck and permitted it to dangle down his back. He opened a roll of one-inch adhesive and handcuffed the judge's wrists behind his back, then walked around him with the tape.

He asked Bobby to finish taping the judge. Lucky beckoned to Mrs. Chillingworth and said: "Come on over here." She came. He placed her hands behind her back and taped them tight. Then he placed a noose around her neck.

"Go on," he said to Bobby. "Take them on down to the boat."

The judge went out first. Lincoln followed him with a gun. Floyd helped the woman down the steps. When she reached the beach staircase, she uttered a prolonged scream. It was the first sound. Lucky did not hesitate. He brought his gun crashing down on Mrs. Chillingworth's head. She fell. He lifted her up, and both captor and captive fell off the stairway and rolled down the sand dune together.

"Boy," the judge said to Bobby, "you take care of us in this and you will never have to work any more."

To this Lincoln had no reply. He was in a position where, if he did not kill Chillingworth, his friend Judge Peel might want to kill him.

Floyd lifted Mrs. Chillingworth into the back of the boat. The judge was helped in. The woman was conscious. Lincoln followed Floyd into the boat and said, "The engine stopped."

It required a little work to start the engine. Sand clogged the pump. Then Holzapfel backed off the beach, turned and headed out to sea. There was a shotgun in two parts on the deck near the engine housing. No one touched it.

The engine heated up again and Floyd killed it and, for a while, the boat bobbed in the late moonlight. The judge's head was against the transom and he could see the lights of A1A. Palm Beach—his Palm Beach.

The engine was restarted, and when they were almost two miles offshore, Holzapfel stopped it again. He studied the shore line, the tiny lights of cars on the highway, and felt that he was far enough out to finish the night's work.

He went aft to Mrs. Chillingworth, lifted her tenderly and placed a spear-fishing waistband around her. Then he slipped lead weights into the pockets. "Come and help me, Bobby," he said.

The men lifted Mrs. Chillingworth by the arms. She sagged. The judge rolled over in the bottom of the boat, took a look at his wife, and shouted, "Remember, I love you." He no longer had illusions about a kidnaping, or being "sent away for a few days." He knew.

She said, "I love you too." She did not protest. She did not beg. She did not fight.

There was a deep booming splash, and silence.

Floyd went over to the judge. He propped Chillingworth up so that he could cinch another waistband. The judge threshed about, twisting his body up the inside of the gunwale. Holzapfel grabbed for the man, but lost him. Judge Chillingworth fell over the gunwale and into the sea.

"Hit him, Bobby," Floyd yelled. "Hit him."

Lincoln went into a panic. "With what?" he yelled.

Floyd said to hit the judge with the shotgun. Lincoln reached down, grabbed the two parts of the gun, and put them together. By the light of the late moon, he examined the shotgun and found it was the one Judge Peel had loaned to him the season before. He had shot squirrels with this.

Bobby looked over the side of the boat and saw the old judge swimming, even though his hands were tied behind his back. He hit him with the stock.

Lucky hollered, "Give me that gun."

The Negro handed it over and said, "You gonna shoot him?"

Floyd said, "No. It will kick up too much of a fuss."

Floyd hit the judge so hard that the stock broke and fell into the sea. The judge still swam. "Grab him, Bobby," Floyd said. Lincoln reached over the side of the boat and caught the judge by the top of his pajamas. He began to pull Chillingworth up into the boat.

"Don't pull him back," said Holzapfel. "Wait a minute." He ran forward and got the anchor rope. He twisted it around the judge's neck. Then he ran forward again and got the anchor. It was a homemade job; a piece of pipe sticking out of a concrete block. He tied it to the rope around the judge's neck.

Lucky dropped it over the side. Then he cut the other end of

20

the rope from the boat and ran back and kicked the judge outward from between Lincoln's hands. The two men threw the guns after the judge. Lincoln aimed a flashlight at the sea. The water was green and clear. He could see the judge and the guns spinning slowly downward.

The surface of the sea was quiet. The boat started back. It was a slow trip. Holzapfel didn't understand boats, and the engine heated several times. Each time he stopped and waited for it to cool.

When they docked at Riviera Beach, it was still dark. Floyd phoned Judge Peel at home. "The motor is fixed," he said. "I'm down at the dock. Bring me a shirt and pants. I got blood on these."

Holzapfel was a man who spoke by lifting his lower lip off his teeth. When Peel arrived, Floyd told him the news about Mrs. Chillingworth as Lincoln listened. "Oh, my God!" said Judge Peel. "I didn't know. Oh, my God!"

A little after 8 A.M. the two carpenters reached the Chillingworth beach house. No one was at home. Before sundown, Sheriff John Kirk announced that Judge and Mrs. Chillingworth were missing. Not dead. Just missing.

They remained missing for five years, long after a court had declared them to be legally dead. They are still missing. Within twenty days of the murders, State Attorney Phil O'Connell of Palm Beach began to receive anonymous phone calls. The voice was a man's voice and all it said was, "You're next to go." The call came late every evening. The state attorney was a fiftyish man with a broken nose. He smoked a meerschaum and said "Yes, ma'am" to his wife. Once he had been a welterweight boxer with a good record. Now he was satisfied if he could get

21

230 yards out of a white ball. His private law practice in Palm Beach grossed better than $100,000 a year and his younger brother was a Supreme Court judge.

In July, 1955, a month after the Chillingworths disappeared, Judge Peel drove Floyd Holzapfel past a Spanish-type house in West Palm Beach. This, he said, is Phil O'Connell's house. The state attorney had bought it cheap a long time ago, the judge said. "It has an elevator in it." Phil O'Connell, he said to Floyd, would have to be killed next. "He is standing in the way of my political ambitions, Floyd. Besides, he is the political boss of Palm Beach County."

Nothing happened.

And yet murder, when successful, is like an ardent kiss. The thrill wears off unless it is repeated. If Judge Peel devised the Chillingworth murders, then a subsequent case became understandable and believable. This one concerned Harold Gray, a respectable young attorney of West Palm Beach who worked in Judge Peel's private office for a little while.

This was two years after the Chillingworths had disappeared, and a considerable time after Judge Lamar Warren suspended Peel for ninety days for telling a woman client that she was divorced when she wasn't. Ironically, this was Peel's total punishment for the Shupe affair. His fear of disbarment caused the Chillingworth murders. Since then, he had quit the bench, and he was talking of quitting the practice of law, but he needed money. Peel liked to live high, and Florida is full of small lawyers who haven't enough influence to fix a parking ticket. Joseph Peel was now a lawyer with no influence. He was an ex-judge.

Peel practiced a little law, but it wasn't enough to stir a small claims court to yawn. So he visited James Yenzer, an insurance agent. Peel took out a $50,000 life insurance policy on Harold Gray, with a double indemnity clause for death by violence. Joseph Peel became the sole beneficiary.

Yenzer was more a shady than a sunny character around Palm Beach. He was the son of a bus driver and, at St. Ann's School, had been known as a good student. As an adult, he was a good student of wrong men.

One evening Joe Peel asked Gray to go with him for a drink. Harold Gray said it sounded like a good idea. They stopped at the Chi Chi Club on Broadway in West Palm Beach. It was a quiet, cool, dark place and they sat near the elbow of the bar. At one point Harold Gray got up to get something from behind the bar—a bottle of soda, some say.

As he stooped, a figure came out of the darkness and beat him over the head. Gray was smashed to his knees, beaten prone, and was still being clubbed when other customers began to run for the door. It was an abortive attempt. Gray went to the hospital, more dead than alive, but he lived.

Sheriff John Kirk arrested Floyd Holzapfel for first degree assault, and arrested Jim Yenzer and Joe Peel on a second degree charge. This appeared to be the end of Peel. When Lucky was tried, his defense was that Harold Gray made offensive remarks about him and about Mrs. Holzapfel. Floyd, outraged, lost his temper. No man can equate a Florida jury, and this one blandly believed Lucky and acquitted him. The charges against Yenzer and Peel were dropped. The prosecutor figured that if he couldn't convict the attacker, then he could not hope to jail the men who plotted the crime for an insurance policy.

This was one of the few times Judge Peel lost a gambit. He had paid a premium on Gray's life, and Gray had not lost it.

Ironically, Floyd and Yenzer got jobs, in 1958, as house detectives in the plush Deauville Hotel. The righteous and lawful

23

job of house dick did not pay much, so Floyd kept a hand in the moonshine business with Bobby Lincoln. On November 2, 1958, Floyd and Bobby had a business conference. Two months earlier, there had been a series of raids on shine stills, and thirty men had been arrested. Lincoln was one of them.

Holzapfel and Lincoln agreed that the Florida Sheriffs Bureau could not have learned the whereabouts of all those stills from a ouija board. Someone must have helped. They thought about it and both came up with the same name: Lew Gene Harvey.

Harvey was a Jacksonville moonshiner who was also in the net. He too was under indictment, but Floyd and Bobby were certain that he was a stool pigeon. They decided to cash Mr. Harvey in. Floyd phoned Harvey in Jacksonville and asked him to come down to West Palm Beach for a conference. Harvey agreed. Floyd said he'd pick him up and drive down with him.

It was done. Floyd and Lew Gene drove down to Palm Beach and picked up Bobby and the three men drove out in the damp, dismal, everglade country behind Palm Beach. They got out near a creek. This was a good place to talk, according to Floyd.

He pulled a gun on Harvey and it turned out to be a good place to shut up. Floyd and Bobby accused Lew Gene Harvey of tipping off the Florida Sheriffs Bureau. Lew Gene denied it, louder and louder. Floyd was in favor of killing Harvey, and Bobby was opposed. The yea's won. A gun was held to the back of Harvey's head and he was dead before he hit the ground.

The two executioners stuffed a concrete block inside the ropes around the body and dumped Lew Gene into a creek. No one would ever find the bootlegger at the bottom of a musty creek. However, Harvey, who had played on the level with these men in life, double-crossed his pals in death. He came to the surface, concrete block and all.

This time, Sheriff John Kirk phoned the capital at Tallahassee and asked the Florida Sheriffs Bureau for assistance. The bureau was set up to assist sixty-two county sheriffs with crime detection, laboratory work, and to act as a clearing house for the local criminal-hunters. Donald McLeod, director of the bureau, sent a shy, slow-talking, gum-chewing young man named Henry Lovern. Mr. Lovern had curly hair and looked like a pushover for a shell game. He looked vaguely like a jaded Lil' Abner.

In truth, Lovern had been an agent in counterintelligence in the army, majored in political science at Florida State University, and was almost as stubborn, on a case, as State Attorney Phil O'Connell. Lovern got to Palm Beach and began to move in and out of shine circles talking, listening and looking as though he didn't quite comprehend anything. One afternoon he contacted Jim Yenzer in Miami. The former insurance agent began to develop a conscience. They talked about the Lew Gene Harvey murder, and in the middle of the conversation, Yenzer mentioned that he knew something about the Chillingworth case. Agent Lovern almost stopped chewing his gum. Not quite. He made a deprecating motion with his hand and said that the Chillingworth thing was of no interest to him; he was assigned to the Harvey case and that's all he cared about.

This attitude forced Yenzer to become aggressive about the judge's murder. The more Lovern urged the man to get back to the Harvey thing, the more he talked about Chillingworth. It could be, Jim said at last, that Joe Peel had something to do with the Chillingworth killings. In fact, if the Sheriffs Bureau wanted a little help, Yenzer would be willing to serve as an undercover agent. He had a lot on his conscience, and he would like to work on the side of law and order. As incredible as it may sound, Yenzer was sincere. He wanted to help solve the Chillingworth murder. He would also like to hang onto a piece of the $100,000 reward money, but this was incidental.

25

Lovern said he doubted that the Sheriffs Bureau would be interested. He listened to a few fragments of information, and left. Henry Lovern hurried back to Palm Beach in high excitement and checked as much of the new information as he could. It clicked. Yenzer was telling the truth.

Henry, the gum-chewing gumshoe, phoned Assistant Director Ross Anderson in Tallahassee with the news. Anderson, an intelligent enforcement officer with skin like a pancake, ordered Henry to tell the story to Sheriff Kirk and State Attorney Phil O'Connell. He also ordered Henry to pretend to continue his work on the Harvey murder.

The Chillingworth case was old and cold. Neither Kirk nor O'Connell nor Lovern expected any dramatic break, and they got none. Henry continued to question bootleggers and bolita runners, but secretly he was working with Jim Yenzer on the Palm Beach murders. Sometimes when he sat in a cheap motel and sleep would not come, he phoned Mrs. Lovern and asked how their four children were doing. She asked when he would be home, and Henry said he didn't know. He just didn't know.

Lovern ordered Jim Yenzer to become friendly again with Floyd. After all, those two had worked with Peel on the Harold Gray insurance case. They trusted each other. The contact was established. The two men made the bars together and Floyd Holzapfel had enormous endurance in the matter of lifting shot glasses. Lovern and Jim Yenzer, a good-looking, smooth-talking, slick-haired young man, reasoned that if Judge Peel had anything to do with the Chillingworth murders, his buddy Floyd should know something about it. What neither of them knew was that Holzapfel subscribed to the closed-mouth policy.

Yenzer asked for permission to join Floyd in a couple of crimes, to win the man's confidence. This too was endorsed.

There were several. The biggest was the night Floyd and Yenzer tried to highjack a load of weapons destined for rebels in Nicaragua. Yenzer kept Henry Lovern appraised of the plot so that the Florida Sheriffs Bureau would not become a party to a felony by permitting Floyd to commit it. The night of the highjacking, Floyd and Jim were watched as they stacked the arms in a truck. Then they were chased by police.

Lovern and Dade County Sheriff Tom Kelly's men stopped the truck. When Floyd got down, he made the mistake of reaching toward his pocket. A sheriff's deputy with a machine gun stitched blue flame across the hood of the truck and Holzapfel lifted his arms. Somehow his confederate got away. Floyd thought that Yenzer escaped by good running. He didn't know that Lovern had given Jim the nod to disappear.

This time Holzapfel needed $15,000 to get out on bail. A one-time policeman of West Palm Beach, now working as a bail bondsman, one P. O. Wilber, put up half the money. Wilber, nicknamed Jim, was a suspicious man who trusted nobody. Still, he put up $7,500. It was his business, and as a bondsman he knew more about the underworld and the business of the sheriff's office in Palm Beach County than any crook or law-enforcement officer. That's what made P. O. Wilber suspicious in the first place.

Henry Lovern went to the Miami parking lot where Floyd had parked a car when he tried to highjack the weapons. Just as he thought—it was the car used by Lew Gene Harvey the night he left Jacksonville.

The state didn't snap a trap on Judge Peel. It acted more like a mother wrapping a receiving blanket around an infant.

27

Slowly, tenderly, the Florida Sheriffs Bureau began to reach for the young ex-judge. No one appeared to be in a hurry. Henry Lovern was still lounging around, asking polite questions. Sometimes he acted as though he didn't understand the answer after it was given to him. Jim Yenzer worked as an undercover man, hitting from both sides of the plate. He was, as the children say, with the bad guys and the good guys.

In October, 1959, a year after Yenzer started to help the state, Judge Peel was in Eau Gallie, Florida, in a business called Insured Capital Corporation (I.C.C.). It promised to build houses and it also promised eight per cent profit on investments. The eight per cent profit sounded to some as though it was insured. This attracted old pensioners, people most easily hurt by failures. One of Peel's partners in Insured Capital was a plumber named Donald Miles. Another was Floyd Holzapfel.

Lovern, the slow-talking gum chewer, was aware of the new business, but he cared little. While Peel was in Eau Gallie working on some investing money, Henry was in Palm Beach working on the bail bondsman, P. O. Wilber. The two men sparred with words. The Florida Sheriffs Bureau agent felt that what Jim Yenzer couldn't tell him, P. O. Wilber could. Yenzer had little more than suspicion with which to link Judge Peel to the Chillingworth murders. His value lay in what he could draw from his friend, Holzapfel. Wilber might have something more tangible.

It was a hunch. A feeling. Lovern, who sometimes played slow and cautious, moved aggressively. He appealed to the conscience of Wilber. He talked like a missionary in heathen country. He cultivated, he cajoled, he contrived, he coaxed.

After a while, Wilber admitted that he knew a little bit. Not much. He said that Holzapfel used to tell him a few things, assuming that Peel had already told him. When Peel stopped by, he used to add a little, on the assumption that Holzapfel had given Wilber the lowdown. When they wanted to talk about the matter, they referred to it as "the 'C' Case" and, sometimes, "the old judge."

In Henry Lovern's head, the little chips began to fall into place. From what he knew, from what he suspected, from what he deduced, from what he got from Yenzer and Wilber, he began to build the image (in his own mind, at least) of a handsome, wavy-haired man who had worn the dark mantle of a judge to hide the heart of a killer. The whole case began to make sense to Henry. He had no evidence to present in court, but he now understood the respective roles of Peel, Holzapfel and Lincoln. He figured that all he needed now was patience.

Then, in December, 1959, Floyd Holzapfel disappeared. One day he was around, the next he was gone. His appeal on a fifteen-year sentence for hijacking was coming up, so he kissed his wife and little girl good-by, went to Washington, and took a plane to Rio de Janeiro. P. O. Wilber, who put up $7,500 of the bail money, could see it winging off with Floyd. His natural suspicion toward all mankind was enhanced by this outrageous double-cross. P. O. began to feel that it didn't pay to play the game on the level. So he meditated and asked to be appointed an undercover agent for the Florida Sheriffs Bureau. He got the appointment. P. O. and Yenzer began to work together for Henry Lovern and Sheriff John Kirk. The Chillingworth case, a dormant mystery for years, began to stir with life. It began to move. Fast.

Floyd Holzapfel had no money. He slept in cheap hotels in Rio and drank cheap booze. All his life he had had confidence on his side. Now, in the morning, his hand trembled. He waited for his pal Peel to send money from the Insured Capital Corporation and it came in tiny driblets. Floyd was a full partner in this business. He needed large sums of money.

A rare thing happened to Lucky. He began to feel sorry for himself. In the summer of 1960 he sent for Mrs. Holzapfel and their son. He missed them. He missed home. He had run to Rio, and he had no money to run any farther, and no money to stay where he was. He talked the situation out with Mrs. Holzapfel and then he sent her home with word to Joe Peel that he needed money—now.

Bobby Lincoln was in the Federal Correction Institution for three years as a shiner. This made Judge Peel feel lonesome too. Lonesome and a little fearful. He was running out of friends. The judge always managed to exude an aura of confidence, but, with Bobby in a federal prison and Lucky hiding in South America, he felt like a man in a small boat watching lightning on the horizon.

The judge, it was said, had taken $60,000 out of Insured Capital Corporation, but he had no money to send to Floyd. This could make Floyd angry enough to want to kill the judge. Peel knew that Floyd could kill without compunction, and he did not want to tempt him. On the other hand, he did not want to send money either. The thought of Floyd made the judge frown.

When Mrs. Holzapfel got back, and got the word to Peel that Lucky wanted money now, the judge worried even more. He needed a friend. Of all people, he made a pal of Jim Yenzer. They had once worked together on insuring Harold Gray; now Peel confided that he would like to have Holzapfel out of his way, permanently. Yenzer could expect $5,000 and expenses if he did a good job.

Yenzer told Lovern. The young agent phoned his boss, Ross Anderson, in Tallahassee and said that the Chillingworth case and the Lew Gene Harvey murder were running neck and neck in the stretch. Anderson gave the news to the Sheriffs Bureau director Donald McLeod, and received permission to go to Palm Beach and work it out with Lovern.

Anderson suggested that Yenzer phone Floyd in Rio and tell him that Insured Capital Corporation was making heavy profits, but that Peel would not send any money. Jim Yenzer did it, and Floyd said he'd be right home. He told Jim to stand by and wait for him. Anderson's motive, of course, was to bring the whole Peel thing to a head at once by setting up a so-called falling out of thieves. Everyone waited for Floyd Holzapfel.

The night he was due in, September 28, 1960, Miami International Airport had more policemen than planes. Holzapfel did not arrive.

Lucky Holzapfel flew to Central America, then to Texas, then to Tampa, and across the state. He was no fool. He checked into the Haven Aire Motel in Melbourne, Florida. The woman clerk was chatty and friendly, but Floyd was unshaven and unhappy. She noticed that he signed in as "J. Kane," but signed his food checks as "J. Cain." To her way of thinking, this was strange behavior indeed for a man who was checking in alone.

Floyd phoned Peel in nearby Eau Gallie, but the judge was in Macon. He contacted Donald Miles, the plumber partner, and demanded that Peel be told to get back quickly for a conference. The following day—September 30—Peel checked into Holiday Inn, a half mile from Holzapfel. This was showdown time.

The phones were busy. Peel called Yenzer in Miami and said, "He's here. Come right up."

Yenzer agreed, and phoned Lovern. Lovern called Sheriff

Jimmy Dunn of Brevard County and asked him to check the Haven Aire quietly, and find out if Floyd Holzapfel was there, under any name. Dunn called back in an hour. "Your man is here," he said.

Yenzer met Peel at Holiday Inn in Melbourne. Miles was also at the meeting. In an adjoining room, the Sheriffs Bureau men turned the recording tapes on. Judge Peel asked Yenzer to execute the contract at once. Jim wanted to know about the money.

Peel said he and Donald Miles and their families were going to leave at once for Daytona to establish alibis. The judge said that when he heard the word on the radio that Holzapfel was dead, he would phone Jim and say, "Go now and pick up the package." This would mean the $5,000. Yenzer said no. He wanted some money now. He got it. He also wanted more after Holzapfel was dead. The judge said he didn't want to question Yenzer's methods, but a disappearance was much to be preferred.

Peel left. Yenzer waited a few minutes and called Floyd. "This is Jim Yenzer, Floyd," he said. "I'm at the Holiday Inn. Come on over. I have something important to tell you."

Agents Henry Lovern and Cliff Powell were in the next room at the tapes. They told Yenzer to shut off the air conditioner; it was interfering with the microphone. Floyd came in, sat down with Jim, and Yenzer twisted the cork from a bottle of whisky.

The men talked and drank for three days and nights. The agents with the earphones next door were worn out listening. They were also worn out trying to explain to the waiter what they were doing with earphones in a motel room. Yenzer told Floyd the whole story of Peel's plot. The judge, he said, had paid him to kill Holzapfel. Lucky steamed, and drank, and talked.

On the second day, P. O. Wilber arrived. He was welcomed like a brother. They sent for more whisky. Floyd waited until Yenzer left the room to talk freely to Wilber. The killer seemed to trust P. O. more than he did Yenzer. The tapes didn't mind. They listened to everybody.

On the third day, Jim phoned Peel in Daytona. He told the judge that he had killed Holzapfel. The judge was noncommittal. In the room, Floyd began to tell Wilber about the Chillingworth case. He spoke in hard bitterness about all he had done for Peel.

Yenzer came back and related his conversation with Peel to Lucky. He had told the judge that Floyd was dead, but the judge didn't seem to care. He was in the middle of it when agents Anderson, Lovern, and Brevard County sheriffs burst into the room. Their guns were drawn.

Floyd got up from the table. "I'm not armed," he said. He held his hands up. Lucky was arrested, and in jail cut his wrists. It was the only killing at which he failed.

On October 4, 1960, Judge Peel and Donald Miles were arrested. State Attorney Phil O'Connell and Sheriff John Kirk were sitting in Peel's old room at the Holiday Inn when the judge was brought in. The judge and the state attorney had come a long, long way for this meeting. The hunter and the hunted stared at each other coolly.

Joe Peel was calm. He was asked to start talking. About what? he said. The Chillingworth murders would do, said O'Connell. The judge said he had nothing to talk about.

The next day, in a local jail, he asked to be taken to O'Connell in Palm Beach. He wanted to make a deal: he would talk, if the state attorney would grant immunity to him. Agents Lovern and Anderson drove him south to Palm Beach. Judge Peel was sure of himself. He made his proposition. O'Connell told him to go to hell. The judge was shocked. He knew that, without the Chillingworth bodies, O'Connell had no case. No corpus delicti. All he asked was immunity from prosecution, and he would be a state's witness.

The judge was charged with conspiracy to kill Holzapfel, and taken to Titusville jail. Donald Miles, the innocent plumber, was charged with the same crime. He pleaded guilty. The judge pleaded innocent and bail was set at $25,000.

The money was raised, somehow, and Peel was released on bail. One minute the deputies had him well shadowed; the next minute he was lost. He walked into a house and an agent waited across the street. Peel was not seen coming out. He disappeared. This time he knew he was fleeing for his life.

The authorities had Floyd in jail in Miami, Lincoln in a federal prison, and no Peel. The newspapers ran stories about these events, and some of the papers reached Bobby Lincoln in his cell. He began to worry about the electric chair. Lincoln was no fool and he was afraid that someone would start to talk.

He asked for his lawyer, a William Chester of Palm Beach. Bobby wanted to talk first and talk fast. Mr. Chester brought the proposition back to State Attorney Phil O'Connell. It was discussed. O'Connell was in a bad spot. He wanted to get Peel, but he knew that if he granted immunity to the Negro, it would hurt him among southern voters.

The case against Peel was weak. The authorities had no corpus delicti; the ocean in front of the Chillingworth house had been dragged for bodies, bones and guns. Nothing had been found.

Three confessions and three defendants would not be as good, in law, as two defendants and one eyewitness to murder. Phil O'Connell searched his conscience and decided to grant immunity to Bobby Lincoln in the Chillingworth murders and the Lew Gene Harvey murder. This was in exchange for a full confession and full testimony against Holzapfel and Peel. It appeared to be a good bargain until Floyd, in jail, became overcome with remorse.

He too was ready to talk. He was promised nothing, but he talked anyway. He burst into tears at a preliminary hearing and said:

"People like us ain't fit to live. We should be stamped out like cockroaches."

To get Peel, Ross Anderson took Donald Miles out of prison. The plumber was Judge Peel's final friend. Anderson felt that if anyone knew where the judge was hiding, it would be Miles. The plumber was used for the final entrapment of the judge.

It worked. Peel phoned Miles and said he was in Pennsylvania. The plumber said he wanted to run away with Peel. They could run out of the country together. It sounded reasonable. Joe said he would be at a hotel in Chattanooga in a few days. Miles said he would meet him there.

Henry Lovern arrived first and wired the room for sound, then arranged with the manager to give the judge the wired room. He could not arrest the judge for the plot on Floyd's life; that was already on the books. He had to get him this time for the Chillingworth murders.

When Peel arrived, Donald met him and the two men sat in the room and talked about jumping bail. Henry Lovern made a good L.P. record of the proceedings and, as the two men emerged from the room, he snapped handcuffs on the judge.

"Mr. Peel," said the slow-talking Henry Lovern, "you just never learn to keep your mouth shut."

The judge seldom showed shock. He showed nothing now. He

nodded to the law-enforcement officers as though they were all old buddies.

The one thing Judge Peel never underestimated was his intelligence. He may have overestimated it at times, but he never sold it short. He had a quick and sure mind, and even when he was confronted with his own lies, he could respond quickly and innocently, and make it appear that people had misunderstood what he wanted to say. If truth is a straight line, then Joe Peel could wander slightly above it, below it, and cross it so many times that no one could tell which part of his conversation was true and which was untrue.

He was taken first to Miami for a preliminary hearing, and then remanded to the jail at West Palm Beach. This was his home town and he knew the warden and the jailers on a first-name basis. The judge was hail-fellow-well-met with everybody, and he made it appear that his arrest was a ridiculous political move on the part of O'Connell.

Peel was permitted downstairs in the visitors' room with his loyal brother, Johnny, and his wife, Imogene. He wanted a lawyer, and he wanted a good one. However, he found that the retainer came high. One lawyer said he would be happy to assume Peel's defense for $35,000, but Joe said he was broke. Another said he wouldn't touch the case. A third wanted $15,000 in cash before interviewing Peel.

The judge insisted that he was broke, although O'Connell claimed that Peel had withdrawn about $150,000 from the Insured Capital Corporation and the judge couldn't prove that he had spent more than $50,000. Still, he was not a pauper and could not go into court and have a judge appoint counsel for him.

He received a sympathetic note from an old schoolmate at

Stetson University, in Florida. This was Carlton Welch, a sincere lawyer with a small practice in Jacksonville. Peel decided to ask Welch to defend him. The idea was that Peel could engineer his own defense through his young friend.

Carlton Welch became Peel's counsel.

PART TWO

THE TRIAL

FIRST
DAY

The trial was held in Fort Pierce. Judge Peel contended, successfully, that he could not get a fair trial in Palm Beach. He felt that local opinion was against him and on the side of the Chillingworths. So the seat of judgment was moved fifty-five miles north to a sleepy town in the center of the citrus area.

Fort Pierce is a red light on the road from Jacksonville to Miami. It is sedate and sleepy, sitting on the banks of the broad Indian River facing the sea. There is more authentic old Florida in Fort Pierce than there is in Miami or Palm Beach or Jacksonville.

It hugs Route 1 like a piece of rock candy on a string. The big trucks run through, headed north with oranges, and the

41

tourists race south in their sedans and convertibles, with money. It is an old town with a whitewashed courthouse and, adjoining, an old three-story jail with two broken rockers on the front porch.

All public notices are tacked beside the front door of the court, and on the ground floor the various offices of St. Lucie County hum with apathy around the water coolers. On the second floor is the Ninth Judicial Circuit Court, a place with a high ceiling, wall stains, a condemned balcony where Negroes used to sit and watch white men adjudicate justice, a jury box, a lighted wall clock sponsored by a jeweler, an oil burner for chilly mornings, some council tables marked "St. Lucie County Property 201," and five rows of benches.

The days were hot in March, 1961. Retired citizens lined up in the downstairs corridor early. The women fanned themselves with the morning newspapers; the men wiped the backs of their necks with large kerchiefs. Upstairs, Judge D. C. Smith began the tedious business of trying a man for his life.

Judge Smith was small and fiftyish, a scholarly and cautious judge with a rich sense of humor on which he sat firmly. He came from Wabasso, a small town near by. There, on weekends, he prowled his citrus groves with a spray gun and sat on the porch in the evening, reading. His nickname was "Bo" but no one called him that in court.

Before him on the bench was an oak gavel. It rested on a piece of marble, which makes a good sharp sound when rapped. The marble listed the names of thirteen judges of the circuit who, in their time, had presided in this court. They were etched in chronological order and "C. E. Chillingworth" was seventh.

The judge made a little speech to the press. He said that he realized that reporters had come from distant places to cover this particular trial, and the court was in sympathy with their work and their problems. He had instructed Sheriff Jack Norvel to set aside the first two rows on the left side for the press. This would give them a total of twenty-two seats. If they needed more or if, at any time, they had problems which should properly concern the court, the ladies and gentlemen of the press were to feel free to see Judge Smith in chambers.

The press would be the only persons permitted to enter or leave court while it was in session, he said. No cameras or artists would be permitted on the second floor of the St. Lucie County courthouse, and if there were any violations of this rule, they could be construed as contempt.

Judge Smith asked Sheriff Norvel to "call the venire" and the prospective jurymen came in, in sports shirts and slacks, silent and slack-jawed, and sat in the spectator section until called by name. Norvel, a short, pleasant man who owned a cattle ranch and was given to orange cowboy shirts and string ties, herded the citizens in politely, with a pleasant word for those whom he knew.

Few men want to serve on a hanging jury. State Attorney O'Connell, big and dark, a man with the authoritative boom of an archangel, looked them over. There were no women among them because in Florida any woman who wants to serve on a jury must file an application with the county clerk.

There were no Negroes either. No one in St. Lucie County looked for any who might want to sit in judgment on a white man. Judge Smith ordered the defendant brought in and the questioning of jurymen began. Some felt sick. Some didn't believe in capital punishment. Some had crop problems. Some had letters from doctors. A few maintained that they had already formed an irrevocable opinion about Judge Peel.

The defendant exuded charm. He sat at the side of the counsel table facing the jury box and he looked young and handsome and confident. His hair was brown and wavy and combed straight back. His profile was reminiscent of Barrymore's; his eyes were hazel-gray and big, with lashes so long as to be almost girlish. His hands were slender and busy and he wore a square-edged kerchief in his jacket pocket.

Joseph Peel was a dandy who could—at will—smile, frown, look contrite, concerned, amused, surprised, courtly and romantic. Behind the scenes he could also drop the mask and shriek invective at his counsel, Carlton Welch, in a restrained whisper. When his wife, Imogene, a tall, dark, handsome woman with long, wavy hair parted in the middle, sneaked up behind him, he could pull her arm over his shoulder and close his eyes dreamily and kiss the back of her hand.

Welch was a slender man who addressed everyone with a drawling gentility. He was young and sincere, and he cultivated a fumbling manner about the laws of evidence and, simultaneously, he worked up a dislike in the audience of Mr. O'Connell's overbearing manner.

The tedious work of selecting a jury continued all day Monday, March 7, and it became apparent that Joe Peel was about to play a dual role: defendant and counsel. He denied this, and said that he proposed to give Welch his private views on which veniremen to challenge, "because it is more important that we have an impartial jury."

Sometimes when Peel could not get the attention of Carlton Welch, he handed a note to Assistant Defense Counsel Jack Rogers, who gave it to Welch. This led to contention along several lines: O'Connell and Welch began to display a bit of scorn for each other; Peel proposed to tell Welch how to handle his case and Welch, in the limelight for the first time, intended to play the part of chief defense counsel and to keep Joe Peel in the role of legal pawn. Mr. Eugene Spellman, assistant state attorney, was a small man with one heavy shoe—he had been crippled by poliomyelitis—and when he limped into court, a youngster with no record, no one realized that he was going to develop as the giant of the trial, the man who could quote precedent and volume and page almost from memory, a man who could outwit Peel without extending himself.

These incidental accidents led to dramatic scenes between the contending parties and sometimes, in the scuffle, the Chillingworths were almost forgotten. The first incident occurred almost at once. Judge Smith said that he was going to lock this jury up in the Fort Pierce Hotel, diagonally behind the court, facing on the river.

At once Welch asked for permission to approach the bench and, having obtained it, and having waited for O'Connell and Spellman to join him, asked the judge how he was going to keep the jury free of contamination if Mr. O'Connell and Mr. Spellman and the Florida Sheriffs Bureau and some prosecution witnesses were all staying at the same hotel.

Judge Smith looked puzzled. He called for the hotel manager and asked him to bring a floor plan with him. The hotel manager displayed his blueprints and it became obvious that there was no way to keep the jury from meeting the prosecution in the hall or in the lobby. In fact, if the jury chose to listen to television, the set was in the lobby and there was no way to prohibit state witnesses from sitting with the jurymen.

The exodus of the prosecution from the hotel began at once. O'Connell and his wife, the Spellmans, Lovern and Anderson and the witnesses had to repack their clothing and effects and

45

find other quarters. No one was in a mood to admire Welch for this tactic, but he was right. The prosecution wives found rooms at the Southernaire Motel, about a mile from court.

In the selection of a jury in a capital case the goal of the prosecutor is to select twelve who are unafraid to inflict the death penalty; it is the goal of the defense to find persons with finely honed consciences, who will magnify the slightest doubt into an acquittal. There are other factors: political, religious, economic, attitude toward lawyers, attitude toward the defendant, sufficient intelligence to absorb and analyze evidence, and an absence of pre-trial opinions regarding guilt or innocence.

The first day closed with farmers and county employees and small merchants bounding in and out of the jury box, challenged, courted, cajoled, excused.

SECOND
DAY

The jury was selected, and two alternates sat outside the box on the right side of the little courtroom. It was hardly a blue-ribbon group. There were two brothers who worked in the highway department; one man who was a part-time minister, part-time street-lighting expert. There were a few who worked farms, a retired storekeeper, a retired coast guardsman and, among the alternates, a retired lieutenant of police.

All of them swore that they were ready to render a first-degree verdict, without recommendation of mercy, if it was proved to their collective satisfaction that Judge Peel was an accessory before the fact of murder. All of them also swore that, if there was doubt in their minds, they would send Peel home, a free man.

47

On paper, the case did not look good for the judge from the start. The known factors were: (1) Floyd Holzapfel had pleaded guilty to first-degree murder in the Chillingworth case and was expected to testify against his old friend at this trial. (2) Bobby Lincoln had been promised immunity, and would come down from the Chattahoochee Federal Prison to support Floyd's testimony. Between them they would establish a corpus delicti as eyewitnesses to the killing of Judge Chillingworth. (Note: The murder of Mrs. Chillingworth was treated as a separate crime, and Peel was on trial only for the killing of the judge.) (3) The Florida Sheriffs Bureau had about seventy hours of tape recordings of conversations by Peel, and about Peel. These had been taped mainly in Melbourne, Florida, in the room where Peel plotted against the life of Holzapfel.

The prosecution's case appeared to be strong. O'Connell stood before the jury to make his opening statement and he wasted no time in coming to the point. His voice was a low Georgia growl and he moved back and forth before the jury like an overage athlete, a nervous, intense man who jingled coins in his trousers pocket, flexed his jaw muscles, and turned scornful eyes on Peel at frequent intervals.

"We intend to prove the defendant, Joseph A. Peel Jr., was a municipal judge in West Palm Beach," he said softly, "and practiced law for several years. We will show that Peel had trouble with the late Circuit Judge C. E. Chillingworth prior to June 15, 1955. We will show that Peel was engaged in the bolita and moonshine rackets with Floyd Holzapfel and Robert David (Bobby) Lincoln, and that together they operated a protection racket . . .

"Peel felt Chillingworth was after him and called Floyd Holzapfel and explained he was about to be ruined. He said the

48

judge has got to go. They got Bobby Lincoln, a Negro, into the picture and the trio scouted Chillingworth's Manalapan home several times.

"Judge Chillingworth had a hearing scheduled for June fifteenth, and Peel was scheduled for another hearing before Judge White. However, after Judge Chillingworth's disappearance became known, Peel did not appear for this or any other hearings."

O'Connell's voice, like a cathedral bell, began to clang louder. "We will show how Peel arranged for the boat in which the Chillingworths were drowned by payment of one-dollar bills from a paper sack, a bolita payoff. Furthermore, we will prove that infantry belts weighted down with divers' weights were placed around Mrs. Chillingworth's waist and that she was lowered into the ocean never again to appear alive. Also that Judge Chillingworth, after sliding out of the boat, was hit over the head with a shotgun, which broke, and then an anchor was used around his neck. . . . Peel and nobody else was the accessory who planned the killing of Judge and Mrs. Chillingworth."

The prosecutor talked a little further, glared at Peel, and sat. This was not going to be a dispassionate, objective trial. None can be so bitter as two former friends.

Mr. Welch stood, tall, slender, a man who often started a sentence, permitted it to die on a comma, and then interrupted himself to start another thought. No one doubted that he came into court believing in the innocence of his client, just as no one doubted that the belief had to be cracked and whittled and, in time, pulverized as damning evidence came from the tongues of glib witnesses.

"After the Chillingworth disappearance," Carlton Welch said, "rumors began to circulate. Peel, blessed with natural qualities,

49

entered Palm Beach County politics. He soon made enemies. Some of these enemies are now ready to testify against him in this court.

"We will show," said Welch slowly, moving his eyes across the faces of the jurors like a man in a shell game trying to find the one covering the pea, "that Judge Chillingworth's death could not have prevented disciplinary action against Peel . . ."

Defense counsel outlined his strategy by claiming, justly, that the prosecution proposed to use the testimony of hoodlums to make a criminal out of Peel. Each one, he said, had something to gain. Bobby Lincoln had confessed to three murders to gain immunity from prosecution. Yenzer and P. O. Wilber were after $100,000 in reward money. Mr. Welch did not mention Floyd Holzapfel, who had already pleaded guilty to the murders without trial, and who might expect a plea of mercy from State Attorney O'Connell for helping to nail Peel.

The first witness, after opening argument, was Robert Force, the carpenter who, with Frank Ebersole, drove their truck down Route A1A to the Chillingworth home on the morning of June 15, 1955, and found a broken bulb on the porch, some blood-stains leading to the beach, and footprints.

It was dull material and the dervish pencils of the press in the first two rows slowed their dance and stopped. The court air conditioner came on like a test missile on a static stand and the judge cupped his ear to hear the words of the witness. Miss Theo Wilson of the *News* said it was the most exciting thing that had happened since Peel's arrest.

Some of the reporters met Judge Peel's wife in the corridor as court recessed at 5 P.M. Her friends called her Eye-mo-gene and she looked good in a two-piece suit. Mrs. Peel was fairly tall and had the legs and carriage of a thoroughbred.

Was she worried? About what? she asked. The trial, they

said. Mrs. Peel had square white teeth and wore dark lipstick. She showed both in a rich smile. "Joe's not worried, so why should I be?" she said. "He didn't do anything wrong."

Outside, the late afternoon sun drew caricatures of buildings and automobiles in blue shadow. A sprinkler on the courthouse lawn flipped water in lazy circles to any blade of grass which might have the energy to reach for it. The reporters walked swiftly around the corner to the old Fort Pierce News Tribune Building where typewriters and Western Union agents waited for the words.

On the side of the courthouse, an old man sat on a bench watching the deputies march the jurors back to the hotel. The judge had warned them that they must not read anything about the trial, or listen to anything on television about the trial, and if anyone approached them to talk or to hand anything to them, it should be reported to the deputies at once.

The mockingbirds in the Melaleuca trees around the old white courthouse cawed and warbled and imitated better birds until Bob Johnson, trusty in the Palm Beach County jail, stood below and looked up. They fell silent as though a signal had passed among them. Bob stood in the late sun, waiting to be called to testify that Judge Peel asked him to kill Floyd Holzapfel in jail last Christmas.

Bob looked like a tired wino. He had a crew cut and buck teeth and the lines of time in his face. Someone with a badge spoke, and Johnson obeyed. He did it without rancor. He was, fundamentally, a good man who had been grievously hurt by life. So he looked at it through the bottom of a shot glass and this threw it a little out of focus.

Bob's job was, until recently, to help feed the prisoners in

Palm Beach jail. Around the holidays, he will claim, a prisoner named Joseph Peel gave him a package of cigarettes. There were ten or twelve butts in it, and behind them, a whitish powder. This, the prosecution will assert, was potassium of cyanide.

Peel is said to have given the cigarettes to Bob, and to have asked him to put the powder in Floyd A. Holzapfel's food. "I will take care of you later," the judge is quoted as having said to the trusty. One can never be sure how the judge meant this.

Bob talked. He gave the powder to the warden. Now he waited to be a witness at the big trial. He may be called. He may not. So he spent a little time looking at the bright blue sky and looking in the trees for the birds who saw him first. They stopped singing when he was ready to begin.

This was a lonesome man. He squinted at the whitewashed courthouse and perhaps he wondered what happened today inside. No one told him. The last of the reporters glanced at him *en passant*. If Johnson had been permitted inside the court, he could have seen little of moment. What? Well . . .

"This young man," said Welch, pointing a long chalky finger at Peel, "will have to bare his soul and his life before you." If Peel took the stand he would have to face the bitter cross-examination of O'Connell. Peel knew law. And he was ready.

Once, the prosecutor was a professional welterweight. Now his frame was big and broad and fiftyish, and it bulged in a deep bottle-green suit. His nose remained broken and his black hair ran down to a thick widow's peak and was parted in the middle. He enjoyed a fight. He was a smiler when he fought. He held his head low and he grinned as the punches popped off his face.

O'Connell planned to hit first and hit hard. That was why he planned to lead his case with Floyd A. Holzapfel. Lucky would be followed by a minor witness or two, and then he would bring in Bobby Lincoln, temporarily out of a jail in Tallahassee. Lincoln would swear the judge's life away and would again confess that he helped drown the Chillingworths on Judge Peel's orders.

Old pals Jim Yenzer, the insurance agent, and P. O. Wilber, the bail bondsman, would attempt to help strap Peel in the chair. They stood the best chance of splitting the $100,000 reward for the apprehension and conviction of the person who killed the Chillingworths.

They weren't pretty people. If the prosecutor wanted to convict, he couldn't expect solid citizens. He was terse and taut when he addressed the jury after the box had been filled. He said simply that a murder had been committed, and that the state of Florida would prove that Joe Peel contrived it. "Can't go skunk huntin' in a tuxedo," he said.

Joe Peel had to smile a little at one point. That was when Attorney Welch asked Judge Smith if he could use his own tape recorder to listen to the witnesses because he couldn't afford a daily transcript of the testimony.

It was a nice touch of poverty. The judge seemed confused, and finally said it would be all right. O'Connell didn't object and he didn't ask the defense, in the name of the state of Florida, to pay for the electricity.

Welch hinted at the strategy of the defense when he said that his young client made a mistake moving into Palm Beach politics. Peel soon found, said Welch, that local politicians were taught that if they wanted to curry favor with the prosecution, the best way would be to hurt Judge Peel.

This pointed up two allegations: one was that Peel did not plot the Chillingworth murders, and was framed; the other was that O'Connell was more than a state attorney, he was the political boss of Palm Beach County. They did not seem electrifying as a defense, but I have witnessed trials where thinner sparks moved juries to acquittals which touched everybody to tears.

Welch drew a final smile on a hot day by asserting that what made the defense of Peel so difficult was the prosecution. This may have been an all-time *non sequitur*.

THIRD
DAY

A small group of citizens stood in the hot morning sun and watched the Palm Beach deputies strike the shackles from Floyd A. Holzapfel's ankles. He sat in the back seat of a car and it was an awkward job. Deputies with huge sombreros had to come in from both doors at once. He held his handcuffed hands high to give them enough room.

They led Lucky out of the car and into the sheriff's office. Court had not yet convened and the elderly men and women were lining up in the downstairs corridor to get good seats. The young matrons of Fort Pierce sold hot coffee, the proceeds of which would be allocated to better playgrounds for children. The jury was led in from the hotel and up the narrow old stair-

55

way to the jury room behind the court. The men wore fresh shirts and slacks; it was apparent that their families had been permitted to communicate with them.

At nine-thirty, Judge Smith came out of chambers, in the upstairs corridor, and the bailiff rapped the gavel and asked everyone to rise. O'Connell, grim and giving away the briefest of smiles, nodded to His Honor; Welch riffled through some papers on his table and glanced up briefly; prosecution assistants Spellman and Brown studied the statement Holzapfel had made when he pleaded guilty.

The judge settled himself behind his pencils and note paper and nodded good morning to one and all. Moment by moment, day by day, his stature was growing with the press and the spectators. He was fair without being grim; he could smile without losing dignity; he sensed that the defense was in difficulty, and in his rulings he tossed the doubtful decisions to Welch; he commanded respect without demanding it.

The state attorney got to his feet and said that he wanted to call Floyd A. Holzapfel as his next witness, but, before doing so, he wanted to explain that there was every likelihood that this man might be hostile and he did not think that the state should be bound by his testimony. In sum, he asked the judge to call Holzapfel as the court's witness. Thus the testimony of Lucky would be binding on neither the prosecution nor the defense, but both sides could take from him what it could get.

Welch opposed this move, and rightfully so. He had no inclination to listen to Holzapfel sit in the witness chair and hang Joe Peel, an old friend. O'Connell made it clear to Judge Smith that Floyd was a man of moods, who was subject to sudden changes of heart. He might get into court, take a look at his old friend, and, for all the state knew, exonerate him.

The judge listened to argument until 10:38 A.M. He then decided to call Floyd as his witness, over the exceptions of Welch. The jury was called into court, and when they were seated, the judge greeted the gentlemen with a soft good morning, and said:

"The court proposes to call a gentleman, Floyd A. Holzapfel, as a witness for the court. The court has reason to believe that this individual has some information that is pertinent to the trial of this case and the individual is being called as a court's witness and neither the state nor the defense is bound by the witness' testimony, but it is offered for what it is worth, and for such interpretation as you, the jury, see fit to give it, and for your enlightenment. The witness will be examined by both the state and defense."

Phil O'Connell looked toward the bailiff standing between the swinging doors at the back of the court. "Bring him in," he said. The word was passed to the witness room, the handcuffs were removed from the prisoner's wrists, and he came into court accompanied by two young attorneys of Palm Beach.

He passed behind the chair of Judge Peel on his way across to the witness chair, but Peel did not look up. Joe knew that Floyd was not going to be hostile to the state. There was nothing to be gained in confessing to first-degree murder and then, when a double-crossing accomplice is tried, in trying to shield him.

Holzapfel sat. He looked like a cross between Mephistopheles, with high receding hairline, and Cyrano de Bergerac, with a big tilted nose. He crossed one leg over the other and sat back to stare around the court slowly.

There was malevolence in his eyes and a slight upcurl to the edges of his mouth. The slow movement of the eyes and the still head were reminiscent of a cat sitting on the branch of a tree, watching a bird alighting. The eyes came to Peel, and locked with the judge's. Joe's head was half down, and he looked up across his own elbow, on the table, to the friend who was willing to face death to hang him.

Sheriff Jack Norvel watched the duel of eyes long enough to see Peel lose, then he checked his deputies around the court. There were extra guards on duty, because Norvel had several tips that someone in court would try to kill Peel or Holzapfel. Two deputies stood at the top and bottom of the court stairway and, at the exits, they stood in groups, smoking cigarettes, guns swinging at their sides.

Upstairs, Holzapfel was going through the routine of identifying himself, telling how he met Peel eight years ago when he needed a lawyer in a false arrest case, and of how he and the judge became personal friends. Peel listened with mouth slightly open, as though by oral communication he could once more get a message to Lucky to stay his hand until further orders.

Holzapfel had a deep crisp voice, the resonant tone of a good baritone. His lawyers stood close to the jury box, listening, ready to object if any question might lead to more trouble for their client. It is difficult to imagine what could be classified as "more trouble" because, although it was known that he had killed Lew Gene Harvey, Holzapfel had pleaded guilty to first-degree murder in the matter of the death of Judge and Mrs. C. E. Chillingworth, and unless State Attorney Phil O'Connell was prepared to ask for mercy, Lucky was aimed for the electric chair at Raiford Prison.

This was a possibility, and Lucky must have entertained it. He saved the state of Florida a fortune by pleading guilty, and now he had come to court to help O'Connell hang Joe Peel. There is no doubt that the state attorney needed the help. He had granted immunity to Bobby Lincoln in return for his testimony, but it was doubtful that a white jury would hang a white judge on the testimony of a Negro murderer.

Besides, there was discontent all over Florida because the state attorney had granted immunity to Lincoln. It did not seem just to the citizens, and even to the authorities, that the Negro was about to get away with three murders, and would go free in a year, just to get Judge Peel. The prosecution's case was weak without Floyd A. Holzapfel, and although no promises were made to him, he had a right to hope that O'Connell would save his skin as he was now saving O'Connell's.

On the stand Floyd reveled in his own venom, glaring at Joe Peel between questions, staring at the ceiling and frowning before answering, as though trying to recollect a precise memory. The lawyers harassed and delayed each other, and fought over little shades of meaning. They objected and were sustained and overruled; the jury was spending more time excused from court than sitting in the box.

The witness told of his growing friendship for Peel. When the judge campaigned for his second term as municipal magistrate, he asked Holzapfel to go out and get money from the Negroes.

Q. How were you to raise the money?

A. I was to contact certain Negroes and others in the West Palm Beach area and attempt to raise money for his campaign, with the promise that he would protect their business after he won the election.

Q. What were these businesses?

A. Moonshine, numbers, bolita, Cuba, and so forth.

Floyd said that when anyone in the police department wanted a search warrant, it was necessary to apply to the municipal judge. Peel told the police that he wanted forty-eight hours' notice before issuing such search warrants. This allowed reasonable time for warning such racketeers as were paying Peel for protection.

According to Holzapfel, the young judge used three methods in the matter of police raids: he warned his friends to hide damaging evidence or he drew up a faulty warrant which would not be upheld on appeal or fined guilty friends a small amount and deducted the amount from what they were paying him weekly.

Some paid $7 a week through Holzapfel to the judge; some paid $15 a week; Bobby Lincoln, before becoming a partner, paid $750 a month. At its best, the protection business earned $3,000 a week. As a judge, the citizens paid Joseph Peel $3,100 a year. Business became so good that in time Peel, Holzapfel and Lincoln set up their own lottery and rented a room behind a pet shop for counting the profits.

However, they failed to protect the winning number. It came up 17 one afternoon, and to pay off the winners, they needed $8,900 and didn't have it. The partners went bankrupt and dropped the business in favor of offering protection to others.

The state attorney resumed questioning and moved directly to the crime:

Q. Did you know C. E. Chillingworth?

A. I never knew him.

Q. Did you know who he was?

A. Yes.

Q. Did you or Joe Peel have any conversation with him?

A. It started in the latter part of May, 1955. Joe told me one day at his office that he had a divorce case for a Mrs. Shupe and that this woman was never able to get a divorce because her husband was overseas. She married another man and told him that she had gotten a divorce, but now it came to the attention of the authorities that her divorce wasn't final. She said that Joe Peel told her that the divorce was final. Now with this story out and because he was running for higher office, Joe Peel said that people were out to get him, particularly Judge Chillingworth. That was the first time I had ever heard of the man. Judge Chillingworth had threatened to disbar Joe Peel. Joe said that an attorney told him, "that squinty-eyed old bastard is going to take care of you." He said we couldn't let this happen because "it would ruin my career and our business." We would be unable to keep them (the Cuba, bookie businesses) as long as he was judge.

The only solution to this problem, Joe says, is that Judge Chillingworth had to be killed. I told him that he was crazy. Joe said, "If Judge Chillingworth gets killed, I have friends to represent me."

We had meetings for a month or a month and a half, and discussions concerning this. "How are we going to do this?" I asked him. "Who is going to do it?"

"Naturally I couldn't do it personally," Joe says. "It's got to be you."

I said, "Well, I'll have to have help. How about Bobby Lincoln?"

"I'm going to ask him." So, we arranged a meeting by phone. Joe Peel and I drove near Lake Osborne, south of West Palm Beach, to meet Bobby Lincoln. Joe got out of the car and went over to talk to Bobby. He came back to me and said Lincoln agreed to help.

Q. Did you know where Chillingworth lived?

A. Not at that time. One afternoon, about 5 P.M., Joe and I,

I'm not sure about Bobby, we passed the house and on the west side of the road, just as you make the curve, there was a man standing off the road. Joe said, "There's Judge Chillingworth. There he is!" That was the first time I ever saw him.

Q. Is that the first time you ever saw him? Who pointed him out to you?

A. Joe Peel.

Q. Did you have instructions before that?

A. Yes, the night of the thirteenth of June, Joe Peel, Bobby Lincoln and I drove past the house to establish who was home. Joe did make some calls at the house to see who was home. This night of the thirteenth, Joe gave me a pistol, a thirty-eight. He told me to go on the beach and look the place over. If I saw him (Judge Chillingworth) I could shoot him then. He let me out of the car south of the home. I went down the path, walked up the back and saw some lights in the window. I was scared. I turned around and walked back. I never went up the steps.

Q. What did Peel say when you got back to the car?

A. He said this had to be done now. During this period Joe and I discussed Bobby and about a crime of a disappearance in Miami. Joe said we could make this disappearance of the judge perfect if we took him out in the ocean. No one could find the body, no one would be arrested. I knew where we could get the boat cheap. [He then referred to a man named Kenton from whom they could get the boat.]

Q. Who did you discuss the boat deal with?

A. Joe Peel, Bobby Lincoln and Mr. Kenton. I bought the boat around the thirteenth or fourteenth.

Q. Did you see Peel then?

A. Yes, every day. On the fourteenth, in the afternoon, I picked up the boat, called to Bobby Lincoln and we took it out for a test run. The agreement was that we were to take the boat that night of the fourteenth to the Chillingworth home, kidnap Judge Chillingworth, take him out in the ocean and drown him.

Q. Who did you discuss that with?

A. Joe Peel.

Q. Go on.

A. On the night of the fourteenth, Bobby and myself, I picked him up at his house.

Q. Before that what preparation did you make, what did you buy?

A. We bought two pairs of canvas gloves, two rolls of adhesive tape, two packages of clothesline, because they sold two together, two surplus army belts, lead sinker weights, but I'm not sure of the weight, one extra flashlight and one extra anchor.

Q. What weapon?

A. I didn't buy any, I still had the thirty-eight pistol Joe gave me. He also gave me his special thirty-eight snub nose, and we got ahold of a shotgun. I'm not sure where.

Q. Where did you meet Lincoln?

A. I picked him up at his house at Riviera Beach and we drove to the dock in Riviera Beach, got aboard the boat and proceeded south along the coast to the Chillingworth home. We . . .

Q. Joe Peel was not with you?

A. No. To establish an alibi, Joe Peel stayed home that night and watched a TV program, the first time I had ever heard of it, *The $64,000 Question.* He said that a police officer had won sixteen thousand dollars that night.

Q. Did he know where you were going that night?

A. Yes.

63

Q. Who furnished the money?

A. Peel did, and we got some from the Cuba. We paid for the boat in one-dollar bills from Cuba.

Q. Go on.

A. We drove the boat down to the Chillingworth home and anchored in the sand. Bobby and I got off the bow. We went up to the . . . [he shakes his head] Joe and I had discussed previously that in case the judge was asleep how we would get into his house. I would go dressed as a boat captain and say our boat was stuck in the sand and could I use the telephone. So I went to the door.

Q. About what time?

A. It was a little after midnight roughly, I don't know. I knocked on the door. This man came to the door. I had never been there before so I asked, "Are you Judge Chillingworth?" "Yes, I am," he said.

Q. [O'Connell presented him with a picture as state exhibit.] Is this the man you saw that night?

A. Yes. Then I drew from underneath my blue sport shirt the pistol and told him to stand still. I asked, "Is there anyone else in the house?" He said, "Yes." He called out something and a woman walked into the living room. That is the first time I saw Mrs. Chillingworth. The judge was supposed to be there by himself. Joe said if I hesitated or backed out "we'll all be through, so if there are any other people that they are to go too." I then asked if there was anyone else. That was all, so I whistled for Bobby to come in, that I had the house under control. As Bobby came in, I heard breaking glass. I turned around and saw that Bobby had broken a light on the porch. Bobby rushed in with the thirty-eight pistol.

Bobby used the tape. He first tied their hands behind their

backs, and used the tape across their mouths. As soon as Bobby finished the tying, we marched them out of the house. Bobby took the judge.

Q. Had you seen Mrs. Chillingworth before that?

A. No. Bobby started out with Mr. Chillingworth and I started off with Mrs. Chillingworth. Off the porch there is the old A1A, then a little to the south a steep flight of stairs. Mrs. Chillingworth and myself started down the steps. She managed to work her gag loose and screamed. At the moment I had a pistol in my hand. She pushed back into me and we started falling. I swung the pistol and hit her. She was bleeding, either from the gun or from falling down the steps. We fell off into the palmetto on the south side of the steps. I was petrified. I jumped up and picked up Mrs. Chillingworth and hollered to Bobby to help me. Bobby had already put Mr. Chillingworth in the boat. He helped me. I then checked to see if I left anything behind. I found that the pistol was missing. I got the flashlight and went back up the steps to look for the missing gun. I went to the place where we had fallen. There I found the gun, picked it up and went back to the boat. We had left the engine idle. Bobby started pulling the boat off the sand before I got there. I had to swim a little to the boat.

Q. What did Judge and Mrs. Chillingworth have on?

A. Judge Chillingworth had on faded pink pajamas and Mrs. Chillingworth had on a nightgown.

Q. Go on.

A. We started out. I was running the boat. At that time I was scared so I don't quite remember. We had trouble with the water pump in the boat. We were afraid the engine would freeze, so we cut the motor off for a while. Then we started it up again. I don't remember how many times we cut the engine off. Finally we got out quite a bit. We decided this was far enough. So we took the cartridge belts and strapped them around Mr. and Mrs. Chillingworth. We threw Mrs. Chillingworth over first. She just disappeared. Then Mr. Chillingworth . . .

Q. Did you put weights around him?

A. Yes, but he came right up to the surface. Bobby started to shoot him but I said, "No, Bobby, the sound of the shot would be heard." I started the boat and chased after Judge Chillingworth. Bobby grabbed the shotgun and over the side of the boat struck Judge Chillingworth over the head. Using an anchor we had in the boat Bobby held the judge by the side of the boat and I got a piece of rope and tied the anchor around the judge. Bobby let him go and he went down.

Q. Then where did you go?

A. We went back.

Q. You had that trouble with the boat going back?

A. We again had to cut off the engine. In fact, I was worried we wouldn't get back. We went back through Palm Beach Inlet and to the dock.

Q. After they went down, did you see them again?

A. No.

Q. Describe to the jury what you saw.

A. I saw the pink pajamas [the judge's] in the reflection from the light as he went down.

Q. What did you have with you going back?

A. Two pistols, a shotgun and rope.

Q. Did the shotgun break over his head?

A. Yes, to the best of my recollection it did.

Q. Go on.

A. We proceeded back to the dock, went to my car and back

to Bobby's house. We were to destroy all of our clothing. We were instructed by Peel. I took Bobby home and then went to a phone booth and called Joe Peel to tell him everything went successfully.

Q. What time was this?

A. I don't know, but it was beginning daylight.

Q. Who did you call?

A. Joe Peel. I told him to bring me a shirt. We agreed to meet in Riviera. He drove up, gave me a sport shirt and we drove in Joe's Cadillac to Singer Island. Joe asked, "How was it? What happened?" I was sick and disgusted. I told him that Mrs. Chillingworth was there. Joe said, "Honest to God, I didn't know she would be there." I just said I was sick and disgusted and wanted to go home.

The prosecutor walked toward the witness. He looked at Floyd and he looked at the jurors. "Why did you kill the Chillingworths?" he said loudly.

Lucky bowed his head and shook it from side to side. Then he looked up, pointed at Peel, and murmured: "To save him."

O'Connell turned his back on Floyd, glanced at Carlton Welch and said, "Your witness."

Carlton Welch should have moved to a cross-examination of the witness well armed because no one knew Holzapfel's weaknesses better than Judge Peel and if Peel, as a competent attorney, had a defense, it was bound to show through the interrogation of Holzapfel. Welch opened by looking off toward a neutral wall and asking the witness if he had not been a member of a college debating team.

Floyd admitted it. The witness was asked if he was not, at

67

one time, a fingerprint expert for the police of Oklahoma City. This seemed so incongruous that the judge leaned over the side of the bench to make sure that the answer was yes. It was.

O'Connell objected that Welch was leading the witness. The judge excused the jury—this was becoming an almost hourly procedure—and gently admonished Welch to stop making statements in the form of questions. Welch asked how wide the door was open, as far as various lines of questioning Floyd was concerned, and, when all the parties were finished nodding to each other, the jury was called back and Floyd sat for more cross-examination.

Q. Mr. Holzapfel [it is pronounced to rhyme with foldsapple, but Welch kept referring to him as "Holds-a-fell"], do you mean to tell this jury that Mr. Peel is responsible for corrupting your life?

A. No, sir.

He admitted that he had been a bookie in California, had been arrested for robbery with firearms twice, served seventeen months in an Oklahoma prison.

Q. You were actually arrested on two charges of robbery with firearms, were you not?

A. No, sir. I was arrested on three charges . . ."

Welch waved a statement in front of the witness. "Has your memory improved since November 7, 1960, when you gave this sworn statement to Judge Robbins in the Circuit Court of Palm Beach County, Florida?"

The witness, who had seemed irritated, suddenly calmed and began to try to sink Welch with cool salvos. "Possibly. I have spent the past five months thinking about this thing and I spent the previous five years trying to forget it."

Q. You didn't do this for pay? You did it for friendship for Joe?

This was a dangerous question. The witness said: "Yes." Defense counsel tried a new tack.

Throughout this interrogation, Holzapfel lifted one knee over the other, sniffed, and glared at Peel eleven feet to his right as though he wanted Peel to understand, as their culminating crime, they were now in the process of killing each other legally.

He was as careful with words as a lawyer facing disbarment. Now and then he closed his poached eyes against a painful memory. The jury leaned forward, tilted like clothespins in a breeze, as Floyd set the scene for one more death.

Q. You went to Rio de Janeiro, Brazil, in early 1959?

A. Yes.

Q. You stayed there until September, 1959?

A. Yes.

Q. Why did you come back?

A. I came back to the United States to one, get money, two, to be back with my family.

Q. Didn't someone lure you back to the United States?

A. Somebody assisted me in my decision.

Q. Who was that?

A. Joe Peel.

Q. Isn't it true that Mr. Wilber wrote you a letter in Brazil?

A. No.

Q. Is it not true that Mr. Wilber wrote you a letter stating that Mr. Peel was having an intimate relationship with your wife?

A. No, sir.

Q. Is it true that you came back to the United States with a lust for revenge in your heart for Joe Peel?

A. No.

Q. When you were in Rio de Janeiro did you know where your wife was?

A. Yes.

Q. Where was she?

A. Where was she when?

Q. When you returned to the United States.

A. She was with her family in Augusta, Georgia.

Q. Did you make a telephone call to your wife and tell her that you knew she was having an affair with Joe Peel?

A. No.

Q. Did you ever call your wife from Rio de Janiero?

A. Yes.

Q. When was the last one you made from Rio?

A. Just before I came back.

Q. Where did you arrive in the States?

A. Houston, Texas.

Q. There, instead of going to see your family . . . What's your wife's name?

A. Peggy.

Q. Did you, as a matter of fact, place a call directly to Mr. Peel charging him with having an affair with Peggy Holzapfel?

A. No.

Q. When you went to Rio de Janeiro did your wife go?

A. No, she didn't, under the advice of Mr. Peel.

Q. What did you use for money?

A. Money from our business.

Q. You testified that the business you were in went bankrupt.

A. Yes.

Q. Then, how did you get the five hundred dollars from it for the boat when this business was bankrupt?

A. We had started another business.

Q. You were in love with your wife, Peggy?

A. Yes.

Q. Are you still in love with her?

A. Yes.

Q. You would try to kill a man who you thought had an affair with her?

A. I don't know.

Q. What about Mrs. Chillingworth?

A. I had a lot of compunction about that.

Q. Have you ever killed anyone else other than Judge and Mrs. Chillingworth? [Objection by O'Connell. Sustained by Judge Smith.]

Q. When you returned to the States, you and Yenzer and Wilber went to Melbourne?

A. We wound up in Melbourne.

Q. At the same time?

A. No. I arrived first.

Q. Then you arrived in Melbourne and registered at the motel. When did Mr. Yenzer and Mr. Wilber get there?

A. A day or day and a half after I got there.

Q. After they arrived what did you all proceed to do?

A. Mr. Yenzer asked to meet me at the Holiday Motel.

Q. They knew you were coming back to kill Peel?

A. No.

Q. With Mr. Yenzer and Mr. Wilber in the motel, what did you proceed to do?

A. Well, I walked in cautiously because I thought Mr. Peel had me set up to be killed.

Q. You were so fearful of Mr. Yenzer that you all started drinking together?

A. Yes.

Q. You mean to say you did that with a man from whom you feared for your life?

A. I was no longer afraid. Mr. Yenzer said, "I wonder if he [Peel] would have killed me after I killed you?" I just said I don't know. He said he got five hundred dollars from Peel to kill me. Peel told him to be sure and get the letter off my body. Then Yenzer went on to say how everybody had been living it up. During that period Wilber came in.

Q. After all of this, he tried to shove a gun in your hand to kill Peel with?

A. No. You have it wrong, again. It was quite a long conversation.

Q. What conversation by yourself prompted Mr. Yenzer to say, here, take a gun and kill Joe Peel?

A. None. We talked about companies Joe and I set up. I had definitely been swindled by Mr. Peel. We discussed past activities of ourselves and Mr. Peel. We had a plan. Yenzer was going to call Peel and tell him I was dead. Then have Peel come over to the motel, get him talking and I was going to walk out of the bathroom. During this period of conversation we found out how we had been damn fools.

Q. Go on.

A. Yenzer said, "Take this pistol." I said it has got to be empty. I don't like a loaded gun. I just want to take my family and get out of here.

Q. Did you hate Joe Peel?

A. Hate wasn't the word. I was completely disgusted with his underhanded tricks, cheating, robbing and killing people.

Q. He didn't throw Judge and Mrs. Chillingworth overboard?

A. No sir, he asked someone else to do it.

Q. During the course of drinking and carrying on in the motel room there, you related certain incidents about the way you murdered Judge Chillingworth. Did you not?

A. Yes, sir.

Q. Unknown to you those statements were being recorded, were they not? [Objection was made by O'Connell. It was over-ruled by Judge Smith.]

Q. You did not know at the time that they were being recorded, but you do know now they were being recorded?

A. I have heard that they were being recorded. I never heard the records.

Q. Did you not say you did it for a lawyer in West Palm Beach?

A. I said I did it for Joe Peel.

Q. You said that on the tapes?

A. Yes, sir.

At the request of the state, the jury was dismissed so that the attorneys could discuss the admission of the tapes into the trial.

Welch: Judge, I would like to examine the witness further.

Judge Smith: Mr. Welch, do you want to make a proffer of your additional interrogation, or do you want the jury in here?

Welch: I would like to have the jury in here and make some further interrogation.

Spellman: Your Honor, we would like to have the original question and answer stricken from the record.

The question and answer were stricken from the record. The jury was then called back in.

Judge Smith: Gentlemen of the jury, an objection to the last question has been sustained by the court. There was no identification as to time and place and those present.

Q. While you were in this preparing to kill Judge Chillingworth I want to know whether there was anyone else involved in the process other than Joe Peel, according to your testimony, Bobby Lincoln and yourself?

A. No, sir.

Q. Joe Peel was not out there with you?

A. Out where?

Q. In the boat?

A. No, sir.

Q. I understand that you stopped out there with the motor running, correct?

A. Yes, sir.

Q. Do you recall whether or not you made the statement, while you were in the room with P. O. Wilber and James Yenzer at the Holiday Inn Motel, that you did this Chillingworth job for ten thousand dollars? [Objection was made and sustained.]

Q. At the time you were in this room at the Holiday Motel you testified you made some statements about the Chillingworth murders. Did you not make the statement that you disposed of the Chillingworths for ten thousand dollars?

A. No, sir. Just the opposite. For Joe Peel.

Toward the end of the day, Mr. Welch objected that the prosecution was trying to keep him from questioning the witness. O'Connell had been objecting all day; Spellman had been popping up and down demanding to know the relevancy of certain lines of questioning. The jury had been in court and out and in again so frequently that some jurors, en route back to court, snuffed out half-smoked cigarettes and stuffed them in their pockets.

Q. You love your wife Peggy?

A. Yes, sir.

Q. You would hate a man who had an affair with her?

A. Yes, sir.

Q. Would you kill a man who—? [O'Connell bounded to his feet to object; the court sustained him.]

Q. Well, you had no compunction about killing Mrs. Chillingworth?

A. I had a lot of compunction about that, sir.

Judge Smith looked at the wall clock. The time was 5 P.M. He recessed court until the morning.

FOURTH
DAY

The yo-yo jury had been in and out of court so many times that now, when the judge wanted to address it, he had to look to make sure that the twelve men were in court. The anteroom was between the witness box and the jury box. The jury filed out, filed in, filed out as counsel for one side or the other asked the judge to excuse the gentlemen.

One elderly man on the jury had found out that his young wife was in court. His seat was farthest into the jury box, so then each time that the twelve came back into court, he displayed his agility to her by bounding across the seats first. In the evening these men played horseshoes together, or walked down on the pier behind the Fort Pierce Hotel to see if the Indian River was still there, or played cards in their rooms. The judge had decreed that, whatever they did, they must do it together and must be together at all times.

This day was spent in trying to make a liar out of a murderer. Floyd Holzapfel was still the witness, and Carlton Welch attacked his credibility. Welch was young, but he was beginning to look tired. He fought doggedly, in the slow drawling manner of the southern gentleman, but he took on too many adversaries at once. Each day, it seemed, he fought the prosecution, the judge's rulings, and his client. Joe Peel wanted to mastermind his defense, and his notions and Mr. Welch's did not harmonize.

The trouble was that Floyd Holzapfel seemed like a credible witness. He would not be shaken from his story that he and Bobby Lincoln had killed the Chillingworths at the request of Judge Peel. Floyd had nothing to lose. He had pleaded guilty to the crime. His answers were disarmingly candid:

"If I said that, it was a lie" . . . "I have lived under an assumed name sixty per cent of the time" . . . "Handcuffs? I've had them on so many times . . ."

Welch wanted to conduct an honorable defense, but he sounded like a man climbing a cliff with a rope in his teeth. Whatever it was he wanted to say, he had trouble getting it off his tongue. Many of the questions which finally reached the witness were hurriedly withdrawn. Sometimes, when he was halfway through an interjectory clause, he stopped and started all over. He had the sympathy of everyone because he was a small-practice lawyer from Jacksonville who, but for the fact that he was Peel's fellow alumnus from Stetson University, would not be in this difficult position.

One thing seemed sure. The defense was not well prepared. It is a matter of common knowledge in criminal cases that, as the prosecution presents its witnesses, the defense must impeach them. Here, the reporters appear to know more than the defense about the sometimes shady background of prosecution witnesses.

To impeach Floyd—which was in the nature of trying to gild garbage—Carlton Welch asked for the minutes of the Palm Beach jury of December, 1955. This was six months after the Chillingworths disappeared. The jury was investigating local rackets. It called, as a witness, Floyd A. Holzapfel. The prosecutor, then and now, was Mr. Phil O'Connell. O'Connell suspected that Judge Joseph Peel was a mastermind in Palm Beach rackets. O'Connell, then and now, tried to get at Peel through his man Floyd Holzapfel. Of course, Lucky had lied before the grand jury in 1955. He may have been lying again, but he admitted on the stand the same day that he permitted a pinball machine to rust in his garage because he caught it paying off.

Welch's idea was to find a few points in the old testimony which disagreed with what Holzapfel was saying here. However, Welch had not read the grand jury minutes, and State Attorney Phil O'Connell, while openly tendering assistance to the defense, was busy tossing a few roadblocks in Welch's way.

The jury was excused. It was called back. It was excused. It came back. The court recessed for lunch, and Welch returned and said he hadn't read the minutes yet. He was given an extra ten minutes, a half hour, an extra hour, and at 4:10 P.M. he asked that the jury be sent out again because he wanted to tell the court that he needed more time to read those minutes.

"Your Honor," he said to presiding Judge Smith, who was now holding the side of his head between his fingers, "I'm right back in the position I was in yesterday. I don't like to waste the court's time. I don't like to waste the jury's time. . . . I request the court to excuse the jury for the rest of the afternoon and I will study the record of the grand jury minutes here."

Judge Smith said: well, all right. So, for the final time, the weary jury dragged itself out.

It was almost a predictable thing that Welch, in the absence of witnesses to prove the innocence of his client, would procrastinate, delay, and either work toward a mistrial or a reversible error. There was no other way in which he could honorably protect Judge Peel.

Welch spent the first forty-five minutes of the court day arguing for the grand jury minutes. When the state produced a copy of the minutes, after reminding defense counsel that he had had four months in which to ask for them, Welch began to question Holzapfel.

Sometimes he asked one question too many. This is common in law, and Welch fell into it a few times.

Q. Did you ever consult Joe on any other legal matters?

A. Yes.

The additional question was: "On what?"

The answer, with a malicious smile, came from a man accustomed to the prison practice of speaking without moving his lips: "On many ways of circumventing the law."

Welch asked Floyd why he and Bobby Lincoln needed two revolvers and a shotgun to drown an aging judge like Chillingworth.

"It's very simple," said Floyd. "If you're going to run into trouble, you should be prepared for it."

The only time Lucky Holzapfel admitted that he might be lying, he put the word "if" in front of it. He was asked about going to the Chi Chi Club in West Palm Beach to buy it. "If I said that," said Floyd, "it was a lie."

Some of the time Welch appeared to be fishing with his questions. Assistant State Attorney Spellman became mildly incensed and asked Judge Smith to order Welch to confine himself to relevant matters.

At another time O'Connell, in a gruff growl, said: "Do you think it would be all right to send the jury back to the hotel for an hour? It's kinda stuffy in that room," pointing to the room. "I'm thinking of them because, later on, I want them to be thinking of me."

On the jury were the two bachelor Carlile brothers, who worked for the State Road Department. Fred, the nervous one, was in charge of heavy machinery and trucks. Hershell drove a repair truck. Roy Cantrell was a part-time minister and full-time deacon. William L. Evers, who listened impassively, was minister of the Primitive Baptist Church. The state attorney cultivated the good will of the jury with elaborate greetings each morning, solicitous remarks about the heat, deep bows when they were excused, and interpretive smiles between times.

The sheriffs were hospitable. One spent three minutes explaining to an old spectator that his seat could not be reserved while he visited the men's lounge. Some of the spectators brought pillows for the hard chairs. One old man in a brazen sports shirt was there every morning at seven with his wife. He listened all day, half smiling and working his gums. His wife dozed with her head on his shoulder. I asked her if she had ever attended a trial before. "He's been doing this for forty years," she said. "Mostly up north. He'd listen to a traffic case."

Visiting lawyers and judges—New York's retired Supreme Court Judge Leo Haggerty was one—had honored spots against the wall facing the jury. Four Negroes were admitted to seats in the white section.

The characters in this drama of callous murder were beginning to show definite identities. Welch had dropped his obsequious attitude. He now asked that the prosecutor "Please sit down when I'm speaking and please address yourself to the court, not to me."

The prosecutor, Phil O'Connell, could be the bully if he chose. His gilded manners and pearly smile did not hide the tough, merciless quality underneath. He was out to put Peel in the electric chair and he had waited five years for this opportunity. If he never won another case, he wanted to win this one.

His assistant, Eugene Spellman of Miami, was the law man in the group. He knew the precedents, the grounds for objection, the bookish material. Even Judge Smith looked to him for precise argument. It seemed probable that Spellman would come away from this trial as the hero.

Judge Peel was of medium height, lean, pale, had almost perfect features and long eyelashes. Like Judge Smith, he was a nose puller. Peel crossed the left leg over the right, and the foot of the left executed little dance steps under the table.

He had personality and vigor. He whispered constantly to his counsel and pressed his points with his finger pointed. His desperate need now was to discredit the state witnesses:

Holzapfel, who had been on the stand; Bobby Lincoln, Peel's Negro partner in the rackets; Jim Yenzer, an old friend who trapped Peel as an undercover agent for the Florida Sheriffs Bureau; and P. O. Wilber, a bail bondsman to whom, apparently, Peel and Holzapfel talked too much. These were all former friends, and Joe Peel was learning that no friends are so merciless.

Floyd hurt him badly in his two days on the stand. His testimony was challenged, but unshaken. He was a liar, a thief, a murderer, but his indictment of Peel as an accessory before the fact of murder stood unchipped, uncracked.

Peel would get more of the same from the other three, and unless he could prove all of them chronic liars, chronic criminals, men who would testify to anything for mean motives, his protestation of innocence might stand alone and naked and shamed.

FIFTH
DAY

There is a monotony to fine weather. Every morning the sun came up over the St. Lucie Inlet like a Christmas tree ornament, and a timid breeze came up out of the southeast and dusted the old freight cars standing in the Florida East Coast Yards, flicked the tops of the coconut palms and brushed the dust on ten thousand window sills into the corners.

At nine, it was always warm and bright. At ten, it was hot. At eleven, people waited for buses under the shop awnings. The high cumulus clouds stood like white caravels in a pale blue sea and sometimes they settled the dust in the streets with a ten-minute shower.

Business went on as usual in the old Fort Pierce courthouse,

83

and business was bad. Floyd Holzapfel was on the witness stand for the third straight day and, although he was through by noon and on his way back to jail at Palm Beach, Lucky managed to survive the final attacks of the defense.

The defense attorney, Carlton Welch, did his best. When he found that he could not shake Floyd's story about the Chillingworth murders, he tried to attack Holzapfel's credibility and in this he did no more than yesterday, when he proved that Floyd was a liar, a thief and a murderer. He seemed, to these ears at least, to be fishing blindly for material some of the time.

The recurring objections of the prosecution to the line of questioning, to its materiality, to the relevancy of certain unknown characters, to the phrasing of the questions, so irritated the young man that at last he lost his composure.

He had said: "Mr. Holzapfel, while you were the owner of the boat . . ." Eugene Spellman was on his feet objecting to the form of the question. Welch tossed his pencil on the counsel table and told the court that he objected to the objections. "At least," he pleaded, "give me a chance to complete the questions before anyone objects." He pointed out that O'Connell and Spellman were taking turns bouncing to their feet no matter what questions he asked, and that now they were objecting before the question had been uttered.

Judge Smith, a Job among jurists, squeezed his forehead with his fingers and said: "Gentlemen, give the counsel the opportunity to propound the questions before interrupting." The prosecution sat, but it had no intention of permitting Welch to continue his case without legal harassment. Of course, some of the objections were not only well founded, but, if permitted to stand without objection, might be confusing to a jury. For example:

Q. Mr. Witness, may I ask you whether you can't swear

under oath that Mr. Craig was in the gambling business or are you afraid to swear under oath he was in the gambling business?

This was objectionable to the prosecution, and was sustained by the court. Sometimes, without intending to, Mr. Welch threw three questions at once at the witness. Holzapfel, the epitome of soulful innocence, sometimes asked the court to ask counsel to utter them one at a time because two of them might require negative answers, and one affirmative.

It would appear that Welch may have done well to skirt the Chillingworth murder in the questioning of Holzapfel, but he kept returning to it like a sick gambler who wants to try the roulette wheel once more.

Q. Isn't it true, Mr. Holzapfel, that you testified that Joe Peel, being a lawyer, told you that he explained to you that you had to get rid of everybody because without the bodies, there is no crime?

A. Yes.

Q. I ask you if it isn't true, Mr. Holzapfel, that that is a proposition you learned in McAllister State Prison?

State objection was sustained.

Q. Is it a fact that when you were in McAllister State Prison you were in the company of criminals?

State objection was sustained.

Q. What type of people did you come into contact with while you were in State Prison?

State objection was overruled.

A. The inmates of the penitentiary.

Q. Then for what crimes were they convicted?

A. [Holzapfel gives a puzzled look and smiles at Welch.]

Q. Did you know that the term corpus delicti is the body of the crime?

State objection was sustained.

Q. Did you testify that you were interested in law?

A. Yes.

Q. Would it surprise you to know that Judge Chillingworth was declared legally dead two years after 1955?

State objection was sustained on the basis of improper type of questioning.

Q. Mr. Witness, you testified yesterday that you had been friends with P. O. (Jim) Wilber?

A. Yes, sir.

Q. Is he still your friend?

A. Yes, sir.

Q. Have you seen him since these charges have been placed against you?

A. Yes, sir.

Q. Did he visit you in the jail at West Palm Beach?

A. Yes, sir.

Q. You say you met Mr. Wilber through Mr. Peel?

A. Yes, sir.

Q. When Mr. Wilber visited you in jail, did he tell you whether or not he plans to claim the reward in the Chillingworth murder?

Objection by the state was sustained.

Q. As a matter of fact, in your suit against the Pan American Security Company, you were represented by another attorney?

A. I think he [Peel] did bring in another one.

Q. Was his name Bill Chester?

A. Yes.

Q. Have you had an opportunity to talk to Bobby Lincoln since your arrest in 1960?

A. Yes, sir.

Q. It is true that Mr. Chester, sir, is the attorney who is arranging to have Bobby Lincoln granted immunity in this case?

Objection by the state was sustained.

Q. In your conversation with Bobby Lincoln had you learned that he gained immunity for that?

Objection by the state was sustained.

Q. Did you have any conversation with Bobby Lincoln with regard to immunity?

A. No, sir.

Q. Did you ever learn from any source, newspaper, state attorney, Mr. Wilber or from anyone with whom you had conversation that Bobby Lincoln has been granted immunity?

State objection was sustained on the grounds it was the wrong form of questioning.

Q. Do you know or has it come to your knowledge that George David (Bobby) Lincoln has been granted immunity by the state on these charges?

State objection was sustained.

In one respect, there was a tinge of the Soviet purge trials in this one. Once Holzapfel got the nod from the prosecutor to start confessing, he immersed himself in an emotional bath. He wrung his hands, twisted one thigh tightly over the other, squeezed his eyes shut in an ecstasy of sweet pain, and the words bounced like penitential hailstones:

"A year and three months ago, I began to think over the life I've led with Joe Peel. [Floyd was in Brazil at this time.] No policeman stopped me to ask me what I was doing. I was in no trouble. When I got back to Florida, I told Wilber that since the Chillingworth murders I had nightmares. I couldn't sleep.

"That night, before the police officers came in—I didn't know they were listening—I told Wilber that someday people like us will be taken out and stepped on like cockroaches.

"I tried to blame everybody except the man who was responsible. I was responsible for all the trouble I was in. Not Bobby. Not Joe. Just me."

O'Connell permitted Floyd to talk. So did Welch. Peel listened with his lips apart, as though horrified that a man could do this to himself. Judge Smith rolled two pencils against each other in his hand. The jury hardly breathed.

When it was over, the state attorney said gently: "Did anyone promise you consideration in this case?" The answer was a whisper: "No, sir." Q. Did the state attorney offer you any inducement of any kind for the story you told here? A. No.

Floyd was asked about Insured Capital Corporation [an investment organization which appealed to retired couples, and promised them eight per cent on their money]. "It was just a swindle," said Holzapfel, shrugging. "Joe drew up the papers of incorporation."

When he fled to Rio, to evade a fifteen-year sentence for hijacking, Floyd's wife Peggy sent him a letter which showed that Insured Capital had taken in $112,000. Holzapfel kept writing to the ex-judge for some of this cream.

At one point, when Welch was conducting cross-examination, Judge Peel looked up across Jack Rogers to Welch and whispered: "Come here." Welch glanced down at defense counsel table and whispered: "Just a minute."

Peel glared up and said slowly and insolently: "Come . . . here!" Welch stopped his cross-examination for a private huddle.

A moment later, Welch asked, as though unbelieving:

"Do you mean to tell this court that you and Bobby Lincoln used to carry your bolita books up to Joe Peel's office on the eighth floor of the Harvey Building in West Palm Beach, and wasn't Mr. O'Connell right there—the state attorney who is here prosecuting this case?"

O'Connell, seated next to Welch, jumped up glaring, and then grinned.

"If I knew they were doing it then," he said to Welch, "you wouldn't need to be here now. I object."

Welch at once moved for a mistrial on the grounds that O'Connell's conduct was prejudicial to his client and that O'Connell was making speeches to the jury without being sworn in as a witness. The motion was denied by Judge Smith.

The defense attorney asked Floyd if, while he was in Rio, he got a phone call from Jack Crane, an officer of Insured Capital. The witness nodded. "Yes, sir," he said.

Welch thumbed through some sheets. "It lasted forty-one minutes and cost one hundred sixty-four dollars?"

Floyd shrugged. "It may have."

Q. You people were having trouble?

A. Yes, Mr. Crane said we had better get some money out of our company. Joe Peel was going crazy with the money.

Welch switched his gambit and asked Floyd if he wasn't the only prisoner in the Palm Beach jail with a television set. Yes, Holzapfel said sadly, it was probably true. He said that someone felt sorry for him because he had been in solitary confinement for months, so the friend sent a TV set. Floyd also admitted that he saw Henry Lovern of the Florida Sheriffs Bureau more frequently than he saw his lawyers.

It was his pal Peel, said Floyd, who advised him to jump bond in the hijacking case and run off to Rio. Peel also counseled Peggy Holzapfel to remain in Florida for three weeks before joining her husband.

Welch asked if Floyd called his wife from Rio. He said yes, and his face began to darken and his lips began to thin a little. Didn't he phone her in North Augusta where she was with her folks? Holzapfel ran his fingers up and down his thighs nervously.

"What was the phone number, and the street address?"

Floyd straightened up, lowered his head, and glared at his tormentor. "I refuse to answer the question," he said in such a soft whisper that few heard it.

O'Connell jumped up, saw the expression, and hastily told the court that Holzapfel was only a man trying to protect his family, and that, unless the phone number and address were material to the issue before the court, he would object. The objection was sustained.

In a few minutes, Holzapfel was smiling at another question: the whole mood had changed. He readily admitted stealing twenty dollars from Judge Chillingworth on the night of the double-drowning, but claimed that he had "left three or four dollars in the wallet. Joe didn't want it to look like a robbery."

Holzapfel said he wore white cotton gloves with elastic on the wrists to keep from leaving fingerprints. Welch asked, if Floyd went there to murder the judge, how come he carried an extra cartridge belt filled with lead sinkers for the drowning of Mrs. Chillingworth. Lucky grinned and turned both palms up. "We took four of everything," he said brightly. "Just in case."

Two other witnesses, a one-armed veteran of World War II named William P. Tennant, and a retired Palm Beach deputy sheriff named W. H. Lawrence, followed Floyd on the witness stand.

Tennant testified that he sold a twenty-one-foot boat to Floyd on June 14, 1955—fifteen hours before the murders—and loaned him an extra anchor after showing him how to beach the craft.

Tennant didn't get the anchor back. "Mr. Holzapfel said to

me: 'I lost it.' " It could be the one Floyd claims he wrapped around Judge Chillingworth's neck.

Tennant, slender, tanned, unemployed, said that $200 of the $450 price on the boat was paid by Floyd in one-dollar bills lying in a brown paper bag. Bolita payoffs are transported in this manner.

Later in the same day, Tennant said he saw Holzapfel sitting with his legs dangling out of a car, sticking lead sinkers into an old M-1 cartridge belt. Tennant asked him what he was doing and Floyd said he was going spear fishing.

Q. How heavy was the anchor you loaned him?

A. I don't know. Twenty-five or thirty-five pounds.

The day after Mr. and Mrs. Chillingworth disappeared, Floyd complained to Tennant that the boat's motor overheated too much. The one-armed veteran said he examined the engine pump and found that the impeller was clogged with beach sand. This would indicate Floyd had beached the boat and left the engine running.

Sheriff Lawrence said he examined the Chillingworth home on the morning of June 15, 1955, and found broken glass on the porch and bloodstains and footprints leading to the beach.

The only humor of the day came when Welch approached Floyd and said: "You appear to be an intelligent and fairly reasonable human being . . ." and Judge Smith slipped back in his chair and said, "Objection sustained."

SIXTH
DAY

A fat noisy breather sat in the witness chair and murmured: "I said to Joe Peel, why did you do the job on Judge Chillingworth? and he said: 'It was either that son of a bitch or me.'" This was P. O. Wilber, a retired policeman of West Palm Beach. He looked a little like Edward G. Robinson and he sounded like an electric saw working through a pine board.

P. O. knew both sides of the law. He was a breezy, grinning man on the witness stand and, if his dear friend Judge Joseph Peel was convicted, the big reward money might be split between P. O. and another dear friend, Jim Yenzer. These two, unknown to Peel, became undercover agents for the Florida Sheriffs Bureau two years before.

92

He knew Peel well, and the defendant stared at him from the counsel table, as though unable to believe that this man too would be part of a parade of pals who had come to hang him. "He began to dig into the bolita and moonshine rackets in 1952," P. O. said in his you-all drawl. "That was when he first made judge." Wilber was a bail bondsman and he put a special stamp on his business cards for Peel's "pushers and sellers" so that when they were arrested, they wouldn't be detained in jail.

Did he see Peel often? "I was in his court every day and once or twice a week in his office." When Joe got into trouble by assuring a woman that she had a divorce when, in truth, she hadn't, P. O. was aware of it and knew that hearings had been scheduled before Judge Joseph White of the Circuit Court of Florida. He also knew that, if the court's finding was against Joe, Judge White would refer the matter to the other circuit court judge, C. E. Chillingworth, for disciplinary action.

P. O. knew that Chillingworth was a strict, humorless judge. When he spoke to Peel about the judge, Joe said: "When you mention his name, chills run up and down my back."

The state attorney never coddled his witnesses. His attitude was abrupt and impatient.

Q. Did you have any discussions with Joseph A. Peel, Jr., after June of 1955 regarding the disappearance of Mr. and Mrs. Chillingworth?

A. Numerous times.

Q. What was the nature of these discussions?

A. Peel always wanted to know what was happening in the sheriff's office. He knew I was in there day and night. He wanted to know what I had heard, if they had found out anything, and so forth. He was in there constantly until 1960.

Q. Do you remember in particular any discussion?

A. Yes, two, three or four months after the disappearance, we had a discussion in Joe Peel's office.

Q. What was the nature of that?

A. Joe Peel was terribly upset and showed fear very much. He opened the door and waved me in. He came up on his toes and he made a motion to me not to talk. He took me to the office next to him and showed me a tape recorder. He slid the bottom drawer out and pointed to it. He said he had reason to believe his office was wired.

Q. Were there any others that you recall?

A. Yes. One in particular. I was in Peel's office. He stood up on his toes again. I asked him why he had done the job.

Q. What did he say?

A. He said it was either that son of a bitch or himself.

Q. How did he say that?

A. That is just about verbatim.

Q. At the time he said that, what was his physical appearance?

A. He was a very frightened man.

Wilber gave the impression of a shrewd man rather than a learned one. He was, one would have guessed, a trial-and-error man, a person who had made many mistakes in youth, and had managed to eliminate them one at a time. Some men without a great deal of education are law-wise, and P. O. Wilber was among them.

For example, one of the small significant items which Judge Peel had not explained was that, on June 10, 1955, he had asked Circuit Court Judge White for an additional hearing before referring the case of the spurious divorce to Judge Chillingworth. On the morning of the fifteenth, at precisely the time the carpenters phoned that Chillingworth was missing from his beach home, Judge White was in court waiting for Joe Peel and his attorney to show up. They didn't.

Wilber was aware of the small sidepaths in law and, although he sat on the witness stand in the manner of a slow-thinking cracker, he was, in some ways, better informed than the lawmen. The most delicate position for P. O. would come when Carlton Welch asked him about the immense reward for the apprehension and conviction of the killer of the Chillingworths.

The bail bondsman had, as an undercover agent for the Florida Sheriffs Bureau, played trapper and trapped, pal and punk; he was simultaneously Peel's dear friend and mortal enemy. The time of cross-examination came and Welch permitted P. O. to skirt the edges of a direct answer.

Q. Now, Mr. Wilber, you are aware, of course, that there is a substantial reward out for information leading to the conviction of people responsible for the disappearance of Judge Chillingworth? [Eugene Spellman got to his feet and said that the reward was not material to the issue before the court. Judge Smith overruled him.]

A. I have never discussed the collection of any reward with anyone.

Mr. Welch asked that the court reporter read the question back to the witness and that the court direct Mr. Wilber to respond directly to the question. Wilber said: I am aware of it. Yes.

For some reason known only to Mr. Welch, he dropped the matter. At another time, to test credibility, he asked P. O. if he was prepared, on the witness stand, to waive all claim to such a reward, but a rocket cluster of objections was fired by the prosecution and spared Wilber the disgrace of being caught with his mouth hanging open and no sound coming out.

The defense asked P. O. if he had ever put up bail for Floyd Holzapfel and Mr. Wilber grinned and said: "Many times. Once, I think, for fifteen hundred dollars in cash; another time five thousand; maybe seventy-five hundred in Miami . . ."

Mr. Welch pondered the reply and stood looking into space like a man who walks into a bathroom and stands there wondering what he had in mind. "Did you," he said slowly, "maintain a place of entertainment for clients at 100 Palmetto Street in West Palm Beach?" Welch had mentioned this matter before, and, by entertainment, he implied a bottle and a blonde.

"Me?" whined P. O. This was stalling, because there was no one else in the witness chair who could answer such a question. "I think you got the wrong address." Welch might have asked him for the right address, but he didn't.

From other testimony, the onlooker was left with the assumption that some of Wilber's friends liked to take sexy pictures. Holzapfel, according to the evidence, was in dalliance at an address in West Palm Beach when P. O. popped in with a camera and made an embarrassing photo and then smiled at Lucky and said: "I just wanted to show you how easy it is to be framed." State Attorney O'Connell heard stories that Peel liked to undress ladies in his office in the Harvey Building and photograph them in the nude standing next to his law diploma.

Welch asked P. O. if he had written a letter for a man named Ted Rinehart. Wilber said yes, and no. Rinehart at one time was on the Federal Bureau of Investigation's list of Ten Most Wanted Men. He was caught getting off a plane in Dallas, Texas, and a search of his luggage revealed a .38 snub Smith &

Wesson revolver. Floyd Holzapfel said he had been armed with a snub .38 the night he drowned the Chillingworths.

"Yes, and no," said P. O. Rinehart, he explained, was a notorious jewel thief, and Wilber had written a To Whom It May Concern note—a note which was never mailed—in which he explained that he had "accidentally" stuffed the revolver in Ted Rinehart's luggage. If this was an attempt on Wilber's part to get Rinehart out of trouble with the FBI it was a foolish thought because, *sub rosa,* P. O. was also working for the government agents.

The acrimony between O'Connell and Welch reached a painful peak when they were discussing a letter written by Judge Chillingworth which told of his plans to take a trip to Europe in the summer of 1955. Welch said that the letter told, in part, of how he planned to dispose of Judge Peel. He followed this with an accusation that the state attorney had tried to keep Welch from contacting Jim Yenzer.

"Mr. Welch," said O'Connell, coming to his feet, "you are a deliberate liar." Judge Smith rapped for order, and the attorneys so far forgot themselves that, instead of addressing the court, they addressed each other. Judge Smith ordered a ten minute recess. When it was over, tempers had abated, but O'Connell did not apologize.

The testimony of other, less inflammable, witnesses would make it appear that the Junior Chamber of Commerce of West Palm Beach had a chronic weakness in selecting its Man of the Year. It selected Judge Joseph Peel one year when he was brow-deep in rackets. Three years later it selected Norman Hart, the young man who rented the back room of his tropical fish and bird shop for the Peel-Holzapfel bolita operations.

Mr. Hart was young and appeared to be a good citizen who

found, to his dismay, that his tropical birds were in bad company. Holzapfel offered him $50 a week to rent the back room on Saturday afternoons. This should have impressed Norman as high rent indeed, but he said his suspicions were not aroused the first four Saturdays.

Sometimes, when he walked back to get a fish net, the young proprietor was astonished to see none other than Judge Peel and Floyd unwrapping brown paper bags and withdrawing colored slips of paper and bundles of dollar bills. Also, there were a lot of Negroes coming and going with packages.

"It came into my mind," said Norman, "what I was actually doing." He was tall and dark and had a cleft chin. "I had to look at myself every morning in the mirror," he said. Norman asked Peel and Floyd to leave his birds and fish. They did. Then the young man became a policeman.

The witness was excused and Mrs. Edna Trepp came into court with swinging earrings. She was a neat woman, a person who might show an edging of gray hair if the beautician didn't get to it first. She was an erudite secretary, with degrees and theses, and she sat on the witness stand with hands folded demurely on her lap, the thumbs rubbing against each other as pacifiers against the ordeal to come.

She was examined by Eugene Spellman, and his questions were soft and direct, as though he understood the tension of a lady in a situation like this. She had been secretary to Mr. Andrew O'Connell, brother of the state attorney, in August 1956, a year after the murders. His office was on the eighth floor of the Harvey Building, where Judge Peel and Phil O'Connell had offices.

Quite often, Mrs. Trepp and Peel's secretary, Carol, had

lunch together. On this day, Mrs. Trepp walked into Peel's reception room and Carol grinned a greeting and said: "Look at my hands. I can't go out like this." Mr. Peel and a lawyer named Frank Maynard were talking at Carol's desk.

Q. What happened then?

A. She got up to leave and I went with her. The men went into Mr. Peel's office, but did not close the door. Outside, I told Carol that I would wait for her because it was hot in my office and hers were nice and air conditioned.

Mrs. Trepp went back and sat in the cool reception room. "Mr. Peel started to talk to Mr. Maynard. I heard this part because I was there by myself. I heard Joe Peel say: 'We got Judge Chillingworth, now we got to get Phil O'Connell. He is the only one left in our way."

Q. What did you do then?

A. The outer door was shut. I didn't know what to do. To tell the truth, I was very, very frightened. So I coughed. Mr. Maynard said: "There is someone there."

Q. Then what happened?

A. Mr. Peel came out very quickly. He said: "Oh, it's you," and I said: "I'm looking for Carol." He just patted me on the shoulder and that was it.

Q. How was this statement made by Mr. Peel?

A. They were like two friends talking, laughing at first. Then he became very serious and intent when he came to Phil O'Connell.

It was another damaging statement, made by a witness difficult to impeach. Mr. Welch did very little cross-examination, but he drew a laugh when he asked: "Carol was going to the restroom and you didn't go with her?"

A. No, I did not.

Q. Had you been to the restroom recently?

A. I don't remember.

The next witness was a lugubrious Negro named Gentle Carter. He slumped in the witness chair until his knees were almost as high as his chin and he got no pleasure out of being in court. He rolled his eyes and said he was a tree surgeon in Palm Beach. He had narrow slit eyes and he told how, in time, he got into the bolita and shine business.

Gentle had a lot of luck, all of it hard. According to his testimony, he was picked up by Negro policemen and taken to Judge Peel's office. The judge asked him if he had been in touch with Floyd Holzapfel and Gentle said come to think of it, no. So Peel told him to get in touch with Floyd, and Gentle said it was a good idea. He went out free and, in a short time, he was part of Floyd's protection racket. This was not too difficult for Carter, but the police were. He was driving to Floyd's house with bolita books in the trunk of the car one night and he was picked up for night prowling, a situation which can occur to any Negro found in a white neighborhood.

The police did not look for the bolita books, but Gentle was tiring of protection which didn't seem to protect. Bail was furnished by P. O. Wilber. Gentle went back to Holzapfel's home and saw Floyd and Judge Peel counting money on a table. Gentle said he was afraid. They told him to get his bolita books and get out. Mr. Carter reverted to climbing trees and sawing off dead limbs. It didn't pay much, but no policeman came up after him.

The day ended on a whimper, and the jury strained to look bright and intelligent as the judge explained the rules of jury behavior for a weekend in the Fort Pierce Hotel. Some of them sucked on their teeth. Judge Smith said that, whatever they did, they would have to do it together: if some wanted to play shuffleboard, all would have to go to the shuffleboard court; if some wanted to walk down on the dock, all would have to go, and one deputy would have to go ahead to clear the dock of any citizen who might contaminate the jury with information about the trial.

SEVENTH
DAY

It was a sunny day and Judge Joseph Peel stood behind the heavy wire mesh of his third floor cell in the rear of the St. Lucie County jail. He could see the jury as, two by two, it marched out of the hotel diagonally across the street. He could see cars go by. He could see the sun rise like a king-size stop light across the Indian River, but he could not see it set.

He thought his trial was going well. He pursed his mouth, lower lip thrust out beyond the upper one, and he nodded solemnly. The trial was going well. The state hadn't hurt him. They had proved nothing except that he was in the rackets, and they had a couple of hoodlums who wanted to save their own skins by testifying against Ole Joe. They had a couple of other characters who wanted to collect a big reward for hanging Pore Ole Joe. Who would believe that humming quartet?

There were two Judge Peels. One was the handsome, smiling, confident attorney. This Judge Peel was seen best in court, where the women craned like birds in a nest to see him. In the morning he smiled at the gallery and nodded; when the citizens smiled back, the judge lowered his eyes and his abnormally long lashes came into view. At other times he scribbled notes to his attorney, setting the strategic and tactical tone of the defense. Most of his conversation was conducted in confidential whispers. His lips and long fingers moved with eloquence and his eyebrows moved upward in a diagonal line. He had the air of an acolyte who had been caught in a brothel by mistake.

The other Peel was a frightened man who clasped and unclasped his hands interminably in the privacy of his cell. The smile was dead. The mouth pulled down at the corners. The eyes darted from side to side though the head remained fixed. The voice was heard in lean bursts. This Judge Peel slid down into pits of despondency. He was powerless to stop it as he went down, down, down, falling, tumbling, always toward despair.

He sat on the edge of his prison bunk for a while, the hands clasped between knees. He got up, looked through the barred door for signs of activity in the prison corridor. He walked three steps in the other direction, and looked out at the broad Indian River, which was prevented from becoming a part of the Atlantic Ocean by a narrow spit of sand.

In the morning he heard the deputy sheriff coming for him to go to court. The judge stopped falling and started to climb painfully back toward the old confident smile. By the time he had knotted his tie, adjusted his kerchief, and run his hands along the sides of his head, the judge had achieved his goal. He was

103

grinning and nodding as the door was unlocked; he swapped manly pleasantries with his keepers; his feet were jaunty as he walked the corridor, preceded a deputy down the two flights of steps, and went to a reception cell behind the sheriff's office.

The only time the judge showed hurt in court was when he saw old friends on the witness stand. When the bailiff called a name, the grin stopped, the head turned, the mouth slacked open in an adenoidal expression and the eyes followed the new witness through the railing, around the council table, to the witness chair.

Today it was Edward Johnson. He was the innocuous, squinting man who stared up at the trees as the birds stopped singing. He wore a face difficult to recall. When Johnson was on the witness stand, Judge Peel listened in disbelief as Johnson answered the questions of Mr. Eugene Spellman, who limped back and forth across a small space, alternately looking at the floor and the ceiling.

Johnson was not a good friend. He was a trusty in the West Palm Beach jail for a short time. He said that the judge occupied Cell 305 in November 1960. His cellmate was Rocky Rayno Davis. The song Mr. Johnson sang today was that, even after Judge Peel was under arrest, he had tried to kill Floyd Holzapfel.

Floyd was in the same prison. One of Johnson's duties was to bring food to the prisoners. On his rounds he found that Judge Peel was a charming and friendly man. Around the middle of November, the judge handed a package of cigarettes to the trusty.

"He said it contained a deadly poison," Johnson said. "He told me that if he got Floyd Holzapfel, he would beat the Chillingworth case."

The cigarette package was partially open at the top. All that could be seen were cigarettes. The closed portion of the package was devoid of cigarettes, and filled with a white powder.

"If you put that in the food or milk," the witness said Judge Peel told him, "you will be well taken care of." This, according to the witness, was a friendly remark rather than ominous.

Mr. Johnson took the package down to the second floor, and there he found a niche between two lavatories and hid the cigarettes. After that, Judge Peel discussed the poison with the trusty "at least eight or ten times" and told Johnson how to put it in Floyd's food.

Defense Counsel Carlton Welch argued against the admission of testimony by Johnson on grounds which might be called peculiar. He opposed the trusty on the premise that he was a surprise witness giving prejudicial testimony, and the defense wasn't properly prepared to cross-examine.

Judge Smith granted a recess, and when it was over, the cross-examination was brief and the testimony prejudicial to the defendant stood. When Johnson left the stand, the judge said that the court would recess for a few days.

The reason for this was a matter of taped conversations. State Attorney Phil O'Connell had about sixty-five hours of these and the admissibility of such material as evidence has always been a sensitive matter in American courts. In the state of Florida, such conversations, although obtained surreptitiously, are admissible if the voices are properly identified and the conversations are pertinent to the indictments.

The Florida Sheriffs Bureau got these tapes—some in a hotel room adjoining that of Holzapfel, P. O. Wilber and Jim Yenzer in Melbourne, and some from the hotel room in Chattanooga where Judge Peel was captured with Donald Miles, his naïve real estate partner. There wasn't any doubt that the tapes were damaging to the defense—in some of them Judge Peel talked of fleeing the country; in others Holzapfel told part of Peel's plot to kill the Chillingworths—still, Judge Smith was cautious and decided to summon counsel for the defense and prosecution to listen to them in the privacy of his chambers.

O'Connell wanted all the tapes admitted as evidence; Welch said he was entitled to hear them first so that he could base his objections on a sound premise. After much discussion it was decided to spend four days listening to all of them, as played by Ross Anderson, assistant director of the Florida Sheriffs Bureau, and Henry Lovern, the agent who solved the case.

It was a long, tiring and sometimes electrifying experience as the brown tapes spun slowly off one reel onto another. There was a dim babble of incoherency, followed by raucous laughter, drunken cursing, a few phone conversations, some startling revelations, the sound of snoring, and an ominous recounting of Peel's perfidy by Floyd Holzapfel.

At one point Carlton Welch looked startled, turned to his client and said: "Joe, you never told me about this." At other points, every one of the listeners, including the judge, was reduced to laughter by the ridiculous language of men who were drunk among men.

Nothing came of it. Judge Smith convened the *voir dire* session each morning at eight, listening to tapes and argument until noon, recessed for lunch, listened until five, recessed for dinner, reconvened at seven, and listened until 11 P.M. It came to nothing, after four days, because much of the material could not be understood; the little bit that was relevant was, by defense contention, uttered by intoxicated men whose competence was questionable.

Smith made no permanent ruling in the matter, and left the

tapes hanging figuratively on their spools. Either side could move to introduce them, or parts of them, at any time in the trial. There was no doubt that some of the material on the tapes appeared to shake Mr. Welch more than Judge Peel. He was fighting an unremitting struggle to save a man whose heart was darkening in color with each passing hour.

Welch lent himself to figures of speech. This tall, slender young man at times appeared to be a lone swordsman backing up a marble stairway, parrying the thrusts of Phil O'Connell, the Florida Sheriffs Bureau, and a host of gleeful witnesses. At other times he seemed to be blinking in the harsh light of his first big trial with stammering tongue and endless interjectory clauses. Always Mr. Welch was the courtly southern gentleman, bowing from the waist as Mr. O'Connell thrust a knee into his groin.

EIGHTH
DAY

A sad-eyed Negro with hair like a tight caracul skullcap walked into court with his manacled hands in a prayerful attitude, and, momentarily free of his federal guards, sat uneasily on the witness stand to save his own life and help hang Judge Peel. For the state, Bobby Lincoln was the most expensive witness in history. He was granted immunity from prosecution in three murders in exchange for his testimony in the Chillingworth case.

O'Connell's unquenchable thirst for Judge Peel's blood led him into an awkward tactical position. It is said that, when Peel was arrested in October 1960, he offered to tell old friend Phil the complete story of the Chillingworth murders in exchange for immunity. The state attorney declined the offer. He felt that the young judge had devised and engineered the killings, and he wanted to see Peel punished.

The state attorney knew, from Lovern's reports of the past two years, most of the story of how and why the Chillingworths were killed, and who took part in it. He could not, in good conscience, excuse the man he regarded as the chief malefactor, just to put two hired killers—Bobby Lincoln and Floyd Holzapfel—in the electric chair at Raiford, Florida.

One of the worst things that might have happened would have been if all three men had confessed. Three defendants cannot establish a corpus delicti in Florida. The best situation, for O'Connell, would accrue if he had one defendant (Peel); one plea of guilty (Holzapfel); and one eyewitness to the crime (Lincoln). This is precisely what happened. Lincoln, in a federal prison for moonshining, read about the arrest of Holzapfel and Peel, and fearing that either of his dear friends might crack and implicate him, offered to assist the state. At the Chattahoochee Prison, Lincoln confessed the two Chillingworth murders, and the killing of fellow moonshiner Lew Gene Harvey. He was granted immunity from prosecution in all three cases.

It was a doleful decision for O'Connell because a state attorney cannot enhance his popularity among the electorate by doing favors for Negroes at the expense of whites. Bobby Lincoln was disliked everywhere, even among his people whom he swindled of their pennies in his bolita racket.

On this day he was prepared to repay what he owed Phil O'Connell. He sat uneasily and spoke in a deep solemn voice as O'Connell snapped the questions at him.

Q. Have you been granted immunity for the Chillingworth and Harvey murders?

A. Yes.

Q. On what grounds?

A. That I'd tell the truth . . . [There was an objection by Mr. Carlton Welch about truth. It was overruled by Judge Smith.]

Q. What else?

A. That I tell the truth, the whole truth and testify that I took a lie detector test. [There was another objection by Mr. Welch on the ground that the phrase "lie detector test" might prejudice the jury. The judge ordered the phrase stricken from the record and admonished the jury to give it no weight in subsequent deliberations.]

The witness testified that he met Floyd Holzapfel and "Floyd asked me how many houses I had selling shine. He said for seven dollars a house we can give you protection. I asked who is we? He said a friend of his. He asked how much do you think you can pay. I asked what kind of protection he can give. He said what kind of protection you need? I said from the constable, the city and the county. He said well, the city you don't have to worry about. He said you still don't know how much you can pay? I said I would find out and let him know. He called me and said I think we can work out about five hundred dollars a month.

"I asked him to tell me about his friend first. I said I wanted to see the man that was giving us protection. He said I was to meet the man that night. I was to go to Mr. Peel's office on the eighth floor of the Harvey Building."

Lincoln said he met the young judge.

Q. What did he do?

A. He went through the procedure of how he would work it. All the warrants that were issued through the city, he would sign.

110

Q. What kind of warrants?

A. Search warrants. He knew the people who were going to be raided. He got a list of those.

Q. Were those in West Palm Beach?

A. Yes, sir. Then he told me that I would always be notified and he would telephone me. I was to give him the five hundred dollars a month every first Monday and it worked out fine. So whenever there was a raid we were notified. If there were any slip-ups, the fines were paid out of the take, the five hundred dollars. If a fine ran too high, he could cut it.

Q. Who?

A. Judge Peel.

Q. Was he a city judge?

A. Yes, sir.

Q. How long did this go on?

A. For the balance of 1954 and part of 1955 until Joe Peel resigned from being judge.

Q. What caused it to stop?

A. He couldn't telephone us about the warrants.

When O'Connell reached the Chillingworth case, the witness minimized his participation in it, and appeared to be trying to give the impression that he was an uninformed, unconsulted third party to the crime. The effect this gave was that Bobby Lincoln was telling the truth, but hardly the whole truth.

Q. Did you and Joe Peel prior to June 14, 1955, have any discussion about Judge Chillingworth?

A. Yes. It was some time before June 14, approximately two weeks. Mr. Peel and Floyd came to my house. Mr. Peel never came into my house, he would call me out and I would get into his car. This time he called me to get into the car. We left my house and went over to Singer Island and headed north on

111

Singer Island. Mr. Peel stopped the car along the road. He said, "Bobby, there is a man who is trying to mess up our business and I want to kill him." At the time we were going to work out the details of how we were going to kill him. Floyd said, "Joe, I got to know details, like when they go and come and what their patterns are." Then Floyd asked Joe about the house. Joe gave details of how the house was built, how you can go up the garage stairs.

Floyd asked, "What about servants?" Joe said there were no servants. Floyd said, "What about their going out?" Joe said that they don't go out very much. He said that he was a prompt man who does everything in a pattern. You can set your watch by him. Floyd asked, "How are we going to do it?" Joe said the idea was to go up and shoot him. He said we would go down there that night. They took me back home and that night picked me up again in Joe's car and we went south of Palm Beach to a house that sits by the ocean. [Lincoln described the location more in detail.] We passed his (Chillingworth's) house several times. One time we stopped, Floyd said he was going to get out. He had a shotgun with him.

Q. Were there any weapons in the car?

A. Floyd had a shotgun and I found out later that Joe had a gun. So, Floyd got out, but a car was coming from the rear, so he got back in again till the car passed. When he got out with the shotgun he went down by the house and disappeared. When he came back he said there wasn't anybody home. We drove to a telephone booth and called but nobody answered.

Q. Who was present during this time?

A. I, Mr. Peel and Floyd.

Q. What was the next time?

A. I thought that they had forgotten about it. It was a week

112

later. I went over to Floyd's house on Singer Island, he had just moved. He was showing me around his house. Then he said, "Follow me, I want to show you something." So he got into his car and I followed him in mine. He stopped on the south side of Singer Island bridge on Blue Heron Boulevard at a dock. I followed him. We got out of our cars and he told me he wanted to show me something. He took me to a boat that he said he was going to buy.

We bought some gas for it and then went out the inlet riding south in the ocean. He said there was good spear fishing out there. He told me he was going to buy the boat and we could go spear fishing. He knew I liked to go spear fishing. Then he turned the boat around and we went back to the dock.

Then the next day he called me and asked what I was going to do that night. He asked me to get off work about nine because he wanted me to go some place with him. He said he would pick me up. When I got home from work, he was already there. I took my gun out of my glove compartment and put it in my back pocket. I got into his car and he drove to the dock. I asked him where we were going and he said he would tell me later.

At the dock he got out of the car and picked up a burlap bag from the back of the car. He took the bag out and we went down to the boat. He said, "Wait a minute," and went across the street. When he came back, he had a package in his hand. It was a bottle of Old Grand Dad whisky.

Then we left the dock and went out the inlet to the ocean and I asked him where we were going and what were we going to do. He said we were going to do that little job for Joe. He said, "Here, have a drink." I said, "What little job?" He said, "Don't you remember?" Then he told me that I was to stay with the boat and that he would take care of it. He said Joe had decided that Floyd was to wear a captain's suit, go up and knock on the door and tell the man that his boat had broken down and that he wanted to call the Coast Guard. Floyd told me that Joe said that his wife "Mrs. Chillingworth" won't be there.

Floyd was doing the talking as we rode on. I asked him how he was going to find the house in the dark. He said he knew where it was. We were going about five miles an hour because Floyd said he didn't want to get there too early. Then he pointed out the lights on the Lake Worth Casino. When we passed the lights we started to pull in.

When we got to the house, we could see the light on the porch. He said, "I am going to leave the boat running." As he got out of the boat he threw me gloves and adhesive tape and said, "I will call you when I need you." He went to the house and pretty soon he called me. I went up to the house, but I stopped next to the stairway banister so I could get out of the light from the house. Floyd said, "Come on." I came up the stairs. Then I thought he said knock the light out, so I did. I went in where he was. He was holding the gun on a man.

He handed me the gun and told me to hold him. When I took the gun a lady was coming out of the bedroom. Floyd put the rope around the man's neck and tied him up in a funny way by bringing the rope between his legs. Then he took the adhesive tape and wrapped the man's hands. He told me to finish binding the man's hands and he went over to the lady.

O'Connell showed state's exhibit pictures of Judge and Mrs. Chillingworth, and Lincoln identified them.

Q. Proceed.

A. He started to wrap the tape around the lady. I said, "Floyd, what are you going to do with these people?" He said,

"We are going to take them out and put them out on a boat."
I said, "What boat?" He said, "The big boat that will be coming
down." We took them to our boat then.

When I got to the boat with the man, the man said, "Boy, if
you take care of us, you will never have to work again." Then
the lady began to scream as she and Floyd were coming down
the steps. He had the lady, and when she screamed, he hit her.
I don't know if he used the gun to hit her or not, but they fell.
When he got up, he brought her down to the boat, and ordered
them to get into the boat and lie down.

We started and the boat quit running. We cranked it. Floyd
said that it must be hot. So we waited and started it up again.
We headed east out in the ocean. We ran the boat a little and
stopped. It kept getting hot. I was standing up in back of the
boat one time when it stopped. I saw Floyd messing with this
lady. I say, "Floyd, what are you doing?" He said, "I am just
keeping her quiet." One time when we stopped, he said, "Bobby,
help me." I said, "What are you going to do?" He then pushed
the lady over the side of the boat. He had been putting the belt
on her before when I asked what he was doing.

Q. Before she went over, did she say anything?

A. On the way the man said, "Honey, remember I love you,"
and she said, "I love you too." Floyd proceeded to throw the
man over. His feet weren't tied and he threw himself over the
side. Floyd said, "Hit him, hit him." I took the gun and gave it
to Floyd. He took the gun and hit the man over the head and
broke the barrel off. He still didn't go down. I grabbed the man
and held him while Floyd took the anchor rope and wrapped
it around his neck and then threw this anchor over the side.
The man got out of my arms . . . it was almost daylight and
we headed back to Riviera Beach.

We had to stop and start the boat going back to Riviera.

Floyd said to throw everything out of the boat. I threw the shot-gun over the side, the rope, my pistol and everything else. He told me to wash off the side of the boat where I had held the man, because his blood had gotten on the boat. We went back to Riviera Beach.

Welch began cross-examination.

Q. You are George David Lincoln?

A. That is right.

Q. As you have testified before, you have been granted immunity by the state attorney for three murders, to appear and testify in this case. Is that right?

A. I was granted immunity in the Chillingworth case.

Q. Bobby, while you were in West Palm Beach, would you tell us what kind of business you were in? I will withdraw that. I will ask you what kind of legitimate business you operated?

A. Poolroom.

Q. How many?

A. Two.

Q. What else?

A. Taxicab.

Q. Two taxicabs?

A. One.

Q. You lived at what address?

A. 1124 10th Street, Riviera Beach.

Q. You lived in Riviera Beach, Florida?

A. Yes, sir.

Q. Can you read?

A. Yes, sir.

Q. You testified previously that you read all the newspapers every day. . . .

O'Connell interposed objection on the basis that there had been no such testimony. Objection was sustained.

Q. Can you read newspapers?

A. Yes, sir.

Q. You would recognize the word Riviera if you saw it?

A. Yes, sir.

Q. And if there was a sign over a dock which said Riviera as you approached a dock, you would recognize that name, wouldn't you?

A. If I saw the name. Yes, sir.

Q. You drove a taxicab around Riviera Beach and you lived in Riviera Beach all during 1954 and 1955, is that right?

A. I didn't drive no taxicab in 1954 and 1955 in Riviera Beach, but I lived in Riviera Beach in 1954 and 1955.

Q. If there were words as you approached the dock from land and you saw the words Blue Heron, could you read that?

A. Yes, sir.

Q. You have . . . You state that Mr. Chester was your attorney, is that correct?

A. Yes, sir.

Q. Did you have any other attorneys?

A. At what time, sir?

Q. Well, in 1954 to the present.

A. Yes, sir, I have had other attorneys prior to Mr. Chester, yes.

Q. I am talking about between Mr. Chester and now.

A. I don't understand you, sir.

Q. Was Mr. Peel ever your attorney?

A. Yes, sir.

Q. He represented you in one case before Judge Newell, did he not?

A. Yes, sir.

Q. He also represented you in a case in Miami, did he not?

A. Yes, sir.

Q. Mr. Hal Ives has been your attorney also, has he not?

A. Yes, sir.

Q. He represented you in a case in Jacksonville?

A. Yes, sir, on the one I am now serving three years for.

Q. Now, you have testified you have been granted immunity on the Lew Gene Harvey case, as well as the Chillingworth case, is that correct?

A. Yes, sir.

Q. How much time do you have to serve in Tallahassee before you will be down in West Palm Beach, or be released?

A. Twenty-one months, sir.

Q. Do you have . . . Despite the fact that you . . . I withdraw the question.

Q. I will ask you this question: is it not true that it was only after you read in the papers that Floyd Holzapfel was implicated in the Lew Gene Harvey murder that you promptly sent for Mr. Chester, your lawyer?

A. No, sir.

Q. That is not true?

A. No, sir.

Q. Do you remember the date Mr. Chester, whom you retained as your attorney to obtain this immunity for you, visited you?

A. No, I do not.

Q. May I refresh your memory by asking if he did not visit you on October 19, 1960?

A. I don't know if that's the right date or not. He visited me several times.

Q. He visited you several times?

A. Yes, sir.

Q. Before January 12, 1961, or after?

118

A. He visited me before January 12, 1961.

Q. I will ask you this, what was Mrs. Chillingworth wearing when she came to the door, when you saw her on the night of June 14, or on the morning of June 15, 1955?

A. A nightgown.

Q. I will ask you this, do you know how to operate an inboard motor boat?

A. No, sir.

Q. Do you know how to operate an outboard?

A. Yes, sir.

Q. Did you recognize the shotgun that you testified was used to hit Judge Chillingworth with on this night?

A. I said it looked like Mr. Peel's gun. I recognized it as Mr. Peel's gun. I thought it was Mr. Peel's gun.

Q. Are you willing . . . are you ready to testify that you say you recognized it as Mr. Peel's gun?

A. It looked like it. There weren't no specific marks to indicate whether it was Mr. Peel's gun, but it looked like Mr. Peel's gun I had kept the whole hunting season.

Q. I will ask you if these questions were asked and these answers given on the twenty-second day of November, 1960? "Q. You said that belonged to Joe Peel?" "A. Yes, sir." "Q. When did you get it?" "A. When did I get the gun?" "Q. Yes." "A. Mr. Peel had loaned me the gun to hunt with." "Q. When?" "A. The hunting season before we went out with Mr. and Mrs. Chillingworth." Were those questions asked and those answers given?

A. Yes.

Q. You testified you recognized the gun?

A. Yes, sir, I said that.

Q. You state you threw all the guns, including the shotgun, over the side?

119

A. Yes, sir, that is correct.

Q. Now you are testifying here that the first time you saw Mr. Peel in connection with this thing was on an occasion when Mr. Peel and Mr. Holzapfel came to your house together?

A. Yes, sir.

Q. And you all went across Singer Bridge?

A. Yes, sir.

Q. That is in Riviera Beach?

A. Yes, sir.

Q. You did not on the first occasion go down and meet Mr. Peel and Mr. Holzapfel in your own automobile and Mr. Holzapfel came over to your car and talked to you about it?

A. Definitely not, sir.

Q. You say it is your testimony that when Judge Chillingworth got out of the boat into the water he did not have any weights around him, is that right? Around his waist?

A. He got out of the boat and into the water. He put himself in the water. He wasn't thrown over. He didn't have any weights on him.

Q. You said the boat was run against him, the rope tied around his neck and the rope cut and thrown into the water?

A. The anchor was thrown into the water, too.

Q. That part was thrown in, too?

A. Yes. The anchor was on the part of the rope that was wrapped around his neck.

Q. How many times was the rope wrapped around his neck?

A. I don't know.

Q. After the disappearance of the Chillingworths did you pay Floyd Holzapfel any money?

A. I never paid him any money. I never owed him none.

Q. I will ask if between the time of April 15, 1955, and the time that Floyd Holzapfel left West Palm Beach and went to

120

Miami to work for . . . do you know who he was working for down there?

A. No, sir.

Q. You don't know Mr. Barney Barnet, do you? [Objection was made by O'Connell and sustained.]

Q. Between the time of June 15, 1955, and the time Floyd Holzapfel left West Palm Beach, did you or did you not give him as much as $2,000 to $3,000 over a period of time? [Objection was made by the state on the basis of the question being immaterial and irrelevant. O'Connell said he testified that he did in the bolita operation. Judge Smith asked that the question be reread.]

Judge Smith [Addressing Lincoln]: If it has any connection to what you testified to when Mr. O'Connell was questioning you, you may answer the question.

A. I have loaned Floyd money, yes.

Q. Did that amount to $2-3,000?

A. I loaned him money several times over a period of time on the grounds that he would pay me back.

Q. Did that amount to $2-3,000?

A. Yes.

The short cross-examination surprised the prosecution. It didn't seem possible that a witness as damaging as Bobby Lincoln, and one with as many weaknesses, would be on and off the stand in the same day. But, when both the prosecution and defense had ironed out simple wrinkles in the fabric of Lincoln's story on re-direct and re-cross-examination, both said: "No more questions," and the federal officers stepped forward and led Bobby Lincoln out into the hall, snapped the irons on his wrists, and led him down the narrow wooden stairway to the marshal's car waiting outside.

He had kept his promise. The dark man had been a sort of

121

innocent, and therefore excellent, eyewitness to two murders. His testimony supported that of Floyd Holzapfel almost line by line, and at long last Phillip D. O'Connell had the case against Judge Joseph A. Peel on the record. He had established a corpus delicti through two eyewitnesses; he had Holzapfel under his thumb on a plea of guilty; he had an off-the-record promise from Lincoln that he would leave the state of Florida the day he was freed, and would never return; and he had mastermind Peel penned behind the testimony of the other two and well on his way to the electric chair.

The next witness was Jim Yenzer, the smug undercover agent for the Sheriffs Bureau. He and P. O. worked in concert to trap old pal Peel. Yenzer was dark and, if one appreciated dissipation and fatigue, good-looking. He dressed well and had a mole on his cheek and a mouth which curved like a waning moon. He said he had worked on this case for Henry Lovern, the gum chewer.

He looked briefly at Joe Peel, and looked back to O'Connell. "In April 1959," he said, crossing one leg over the other, "I told Peel that I knew of his participation in the Chillingworth murders. I told him that Floyd had told me. Joe said that Floyd should be careful who he talks to." This was hardly an admission of guilt, but Yenzer stood a chance of getting some of the $100,000 reward money for the apprehension and conviction of the murderer or murderers of Judge and Mrs. Chillingworth, and he could hardly be expected to minimize his work. Later, Yenzer told Peel that Floyd would be a threat "if he ever starts talking." Peel said: "I know. I know."

The judge was getting angry messages from Floyd in the autumn of 1959 about Holzapfel's share of the Eau Gallie real estate swindle when Peel "asked me if I would kill Floyd Holzapfel. I told Joe that when and if he decided to hit Floyd to let me know definitely. Later he asked if I would kill for him. I said yes. He said how much would I charge. I said: 'Normally, five to ten thousand.' He said he might go for two thousand."

The ex-judge asked Yenzer if he knew how to use a boat, that it would look better as a kidnaping. If Peel made this suggestion, he was in a rut. Also, he would be playing into the hands of Yenzer. Still, if Peel devised the murders of the Chillingworths, then, after five years of freedom, or lack of detection, one can understand why he would want all murders to follow the successful pattern.

By November 1959 the fee was inched to $3,000, then $3,300. The judge eventually moved it up to $5,300, provided that Jim Yenzer paid $2,000 of it to an assistant murderer. Ironically, Peel eventually paid most of this money to Yenzer, who reported every dollar of it, and every word out of Peel's mouth, to Sheriffs Agent Henry Lovern. Yenzer was playing for higher stakes.

All this time, Mr. Holzapfel was hiding from the law in Rio de Janeiro. He was alone and he was bitter. His wife was back in the United States; so too was his quiet pride, his little girl; Floyd, who felt that he had done no more wrong than his friend the judge, had no home, no car, no money, no friends, in addition to which his dear friend and partner, Joe Peel, was holding out money obtained in the Eau Gallie real estate swindle.

In the last days of September 1960, Jim Yenzer went up to Coco Beach and met Judge Peel at a motel. The judge was nervous. He kept kicking the drapes aside and looking behind them. When he wasn't doing that, he was lifting lamps and shaking the bases. After a while, he asked Jim to step outside for a talk.

The afternoon sun fixed their faces in gold as they chatted. Yenzer wanted to talk about the Chillingworth murders; Peel wanted to discuss the projected murder of Floyd Holzapfel. Yenzer said that the authorities down at Palm Beach were offering $100,000 for the bones of the Chillingworths.

The judge grinned and shook his head. He said that if a man was to take a boat and sail it from the center of the Chillingworth property due east, about a hundred yards beyond the southbound steamer track, he would find the bodies. Or what was left of them after five years.

A few days later, Peel and Yenzer completed the plot to kill Floyd. Donald Miles, the plumber partner, was in the room at the time. This was a surprise because, until Mr. Miles met the judge, he had been a law-abiding citizen.

They were in Room 127 of a local motel in Melbourne. In the next room, Agent Lovern and an assistant tested their earphones and tapes. Some of the sound came through clearly, but only when the three men in the next room were near the microphone. Sometimes, when the tapes were spinning well, an air conditioner cut in and all the words were buried under a hum.

Miles discussed something which the other two knew: that Floyd Holzapfel had left his hideaway in South America and was now in a motel only a half mile away, looking for Judge Peel. Miles said that he had visited Floyd and that Holzapfel was "going to tell about the Chillingworth case."

The judge said that Floyd was a raving maniac. They talked a while, and Yenzer asked Miles if he would leave the room for a moment because he wanted to discuss some private business with Peel. Miles withdrew, and Yenzer said he had a private worry. "After I kill Floyd," he said, "the other persons in the

Chillingworth thing will come looking for me. What can I do to protect myself?"

Yenzer, of course, had no intention of killing Holzapfel. He pretended to become a party to the plot so that he could win the confidence of the judge and find out more about the Chillingworth case. He was now trying to ascertain how many others had been parties to it. "Don't worry," Judge Peel said, "the other person is in the penitentiary."

The undercover agent now realized that there had been three persons in the conspiracy: the judge, Floyd, and someone who was in prison. It wouldn't be difficult to find out who, among Peel's friends, was in a penitentiary. Besides, the strategy of pitting Floyd against the judge, and the judge against Floyd, was bound to lead to further disclosures soon because Floyd was in town to collect money promised by Peel, and Peel, fearful of his life, was plotting to kill Floyd.

O'Connell turned the witness over to Welch, and the defense counsel tried to impeach Yenzer on the reward money. It seemed obvious that this man expected a part of the money for his work, and Welch handled this impeachment skillfully. He then asked the witness a dangerous question: "Did Peel ever admit to you anything about the Chillingworth murders?"

"He never came out and told me he did it," said Jim Yenzer, "but when I said I knew his part in it he said: 'I know. I know.' "

Both sides excused the witness. Judge Smith nodded to Sheriff Jack Norvel and he rapped a gavel on the court railing and announced that court had recessed until the morning. The judge swept out through the gate, the citizens in the five rows of spectators' benches stood until he disappeared in his chambers. O'Connell glanced around the court, whispered to Spellman, and packed his briefcase for the day. Welch sat, running his hands through his thick hair, the features sagging downward from the courtly smile toward solemn depression. Judge Peel sat rolling a pencil back and forth under his fingers. He nodded to the sheriff that he was ready to go back to jail whenever the deputies were. The reporters finished penciling a final note or two, then started to walk out in small groups, to go down the steps to the ground floor, out the side door, across the parking lot and around the corner to the old Fort Pierce News Tribune Building, where there were typewriters and Western Union operators.

In ten minutes the court was empty. It looked dusty and old with its rusty wall stains, the jeweler's clock over the stove, and the council tables with their individual indentifications: "Prop. of St. Lucie County 201." Suddenly the big ceiling fan went on. It was the only wind that boded anybody any good.

NINTH DAY

The aplomb of the defendant was gone. It left that morning. The smile died while a young witness named Rayno E. Davis was testifying. The mouth was now turned down, and hung slightly open. The twinkling eyes now stared in silent fear. A finger on the council table drew interminable figure eights. Judge Peel looked older.

Rayno (Rocky) Davis was nineteen. He was serving a sentence for grand larceny in Palm Beach jail. Last November he had drawn Judge Peel as a cellmate. Rayno Davis, as a first offender, looked up to Peel in awe. Peel, if one can believe the boy's testimony, showed Davis a package of cigarettes and said it contained deadly poison. He also told the youngster that it was intended for Floyd Holzapfel's dinner.

This, of course, amounted to suitable corroboration of Mr. Johnson's singing story about the poison. It also tended to show that, in confinement, the judge was prone to mental lapses. He could have no motive in telling this boy about the cigarettes other than trying to provide Phil O'Connell with an additional witness.

Young Davis also testified to the most hilarious jail break in history. He said that he and the judge plotted to break out of Palm Beach jail except that, on the night that it was scheduled, Peel forgot to join him. The break, as planned, was a libel on the sheriff's guards, because Peel and Rayno planned to walk out when the jail visitors were leaving.

Davis walked out and, when he got on the lawn, he waited for the judge, but neither Peel nor the deputies bothered to come out. The judge had promised Davis a get-away car, and the kid began to bet himself that the car wouldn't be there. It wasn't. He hitchhiked all the way to Jacksonville and then, disillusioned, gave himself up.

Rocky had jet wavy hair and a Cupid's bow mouth. His skin was as pale as talcum. He was confused, not evil. He said he had escaped because he had a young bride and, in spite of his mistake (breaking and entering), she believed in him and he was impatient to rejoin her. When young Mr. Davis gave himself up, he figuratively bailed the sheriff out of a lot of trouble. In gratitude, the sheriff could not free Rayno, but he did the next best thing: he got young Mrs. Davis a job in the prison.

When Davis went back to jail after cross-examination, J. Donald Miles was called to the witness stand. This case was replete with supposedly nice people who were derailed by Peel. Miles had a dark shoebrush on his head. He was thirty and until he met the judge he was an average plumber in Eau Gallie,

Florida. Fourteen months later he was helping Peel to plot the murder of Floyd Holzapfel.

Miles looked as naïve as a high-school boy delivering towels to a bordello. The judge set up an organization called Insured Capital, which was neither of those words, and made Miles a partner. Lucky Holzapfel was another partner. The idea was to go into the building business up around Melbourne, buy some lots, build a few houses, and then advertise for investors and promise eight per cent interest.

It is not a new scheme. It has been abused before. Most of the suckers are usually retired grandparents who have what they refer to as a little nest egg. They see an opportunity to make a bigger one out of it and they exchange the egg for something which looks like a stock certificate but which, when stripped of its legal semantics, is a promissory note.

Donald Miles found himself charmed out of his pipes and wrenches by Joe Peel. He was willing to take direction from Joe. His respect for Peel's intelligence was predicated on his appreciation of his own lack of it. When Miles sat in the witness box and smoothed the crease in his trousers, the defendant began to shake his head no and to mutter and write notes to himself.

State Attorney Phil O'Connell took Miles right to the nub of his story. Miles said that on the final day of September, 1960, he and Peel and Jim Yenzer were in Room 127 at the Holiday Inn in Melbourne. Peel asked Yenzer to go down the road to the Haven Aire Motel, Room 26, and kill Floyd Holzapfel.

"I intend to get Floyd out of the way," said Peel, as quoted by Miles, "because he has enough on me to put me in the electric chair.

"Do you have anyone to help you?" Peel said to Yenzer. The

undercover agent nodded. "I have a man from Jacksonville," he said. Peel beamed happily. "I love you," he murmured. "I hope everything goes all right."

Miles, who admitted being present and would be sentenced for being a party to all this, said that Peel wanted to leave Holiday Inn the moment Yenzer was ready to kill Floyd. He took his wife; so did Miles. They went to Daytona Beach to establish an alibi. Before Yenzer left, he phoned Peel's younger brother, John, to ask the latest news about Floyd's disposition.

Yenzer said to the judge: "Johnny said he is going to Holzapfel's to have a drink." Miles said: "Suppose Johnny is there when Jim Yenzer arrives?" The judge shook his head sadly. "Then," he said succinctly, "Jim will have to take him too." Cain could not have uttered the words with less malice, and more love.

The two families went off to Daytona. Peel was devoted to the news broadcasts on television and he expected to hear an announcement that "Floyd A. Holzapfel, a Florida convict, was found shot to death in a Melbourne motel under mysterious circumstances today." He tuned in all day and all evening, but the announcement never came.

Instead, on the third evening, a news announcer said: "Floyd A. Holzapfel, a Florida criminal, was arrested today and police claim that the five-year-old mystery disappearance of Circuit Judge and Mrs. C. E. Chillingworth is now cleared up."

Peel, said Mr. Miles, became agitated and the two families fled to Macon, Georgia. When they arrived, the judge asked Don casually if he could get some poison. The question worried Miles because he was learning that, when Joe asked a question like that, it required a sharp mentality to divine who was going to get it.

The judge put Don at ease. He said he wanted to commit suicide. Then, before Donald could answer the question, Peel said that suicide by poison was out of the question because it would present insurance difficulties for Imogene, his wife. "I'd better get on a plane," Joe said casually, "and blow it up. Do you know anything about making a bomb?" Miles did not. He didn't even know much about fleeing, because, a few weeks later, he and Judge Peel were trapped by the law in a small hotel in Chattanooga.

At 3 P.M. O'Connell turned the witness over to Welch for cross-examination. The defense counsel had some questions, but they did not shake the story of the witness. At 3:43 P.M., Mr. O'Connell got to his feet and said: "The state rests, your honor."

Welch then made a motion for a directed verdict of acquittal on the grounds that the state had not adduced sufficient evidence to establish a prima facie case against Joseph A. Peel. Judge Smith listened patiently, nodding a little at the familiar empty words, and then, softly and undramatically, said, "Motion denied."

Defense counsel then told reporters that Peel would be his main witness.

TENTH
DAY

The defense opened like the second act of *Guys and Dolls*. There was decorum in the courtroom until Mr. Welch called the name "John Tedesco." Mr. Tedesco, a short, gray-haired bartender, steamed into the witness chair like a runaway kettle. He glared at one and all angrily and said that he had overheard the late Barney Barnet ask Floyd Holzapfel to "do a job in Palm Beach"—the implication being that Mr. Barnet asked Floyd to kill the Chillingworths.

This, of course, would tend to support Lucky's confession while, at the same time, removing Judge Peel from the role of mastermind and replacing him with a man now dead. This is, at best, a risky gambit, very much in the nature of taking dead aim on a charging elephant with a jammed beebee gun. Before Tedesco testified, Defense Counsel Welch made a *voir dire* proffer of the testimony.

Many attorneys do not always use English as a form of communication. Sometimes they abuse words, bruise them, and, in their anxiety to adduce facts, confuse everyone. One of Mr. Welch's introductory sentences in relation to Mr. Tedesco was a marvel of linguistic judo.

"We state to the court that this witness has stated to me that he in the month of January 1955, after this witness was a bartender at the club in Miami, that he overheard a conversation between Floyd Holzapfel and Barney Barnet and that this witness was also in the employment of Barney Barnet and at that time and that place he heard Floyd Holzapfel and Barnet discussing a contract for a man who was having an argument with Judge Chillingworth about the custody of some children, to kill the judge."

Welch took a breath, the judge rubbed his forehead with his finger tips, and defense counsel continued. "This witness will testify to the fact that in the latter part of June 1955, he went to the home of Barney Barnet and there was some discussion about a boat ride and that Barney Barnet had a boat and that boat had a cabin on the front. Barney Barnet said he was having the boat repaired and told them to come back in July. The first time I ever heard of this witness is when he came to Jacksonville looking for me. He said he grew up with Floyd Holzapfel and knew Barney Barnet. I request to the court that we have Floyd Holzapfel present so the witness can identify him. I feel that he should be brought as a court's witness."

Welch asked that Tedesco be called as a court's witness. This was denied. The defense called him as its own, and O'Connell

133

stood and growled: "If they are talking about someone else who wanted Judge Chillingworth killed, there must be more evidence."

Judge Smith agreed and Welch said he would proffer Tedesco from the witness stand out of the hearing of the jury. The witness sat, just breathing and steaming up the glasses of counsel. Welch worked him around his name and occupation, and his friendship with Mr. Barnet and Mr. Holzapfel, toward a conversation in the Harem Club at Miami Beach in the spring of 1955.

"I only caught snatches of it," said Mr. Tedesco. "They had a big deal cookin' in West Palm Beach. They were supposed to take care of somebody. Something that involved an adoption case. He was looking for somebody to do something for him."

This was uttered in a Hoboken patois, and it related to a discussion between Floyd and Barnet.

Q. Did you hear the name of Joe Peel mentioned?

A. Yeah.

Q. What was said about that?

A. Well, we was coming to West Palm Beach the time Barney was getting a club, the Rag Doll. We were told to get outta town. [Mr. Spellman interrupted: "You lost the time and place."]

Q. Do you know when that conversation was?

A. That was no conversation. You asked me when I heard Joe Peel mentioned. This was in a bar when Lucky come in and tried to steam me up. He knew I steam easy. He was steamed that Joe Peel was fooling around with his old lady. Lucky asked me if I wanted to give Peel a workout. I said what the hell's the difference. I said don't believe everything you hear. Anyway, I got troubles of my own.

134

Q. You mean Floyd Holzapfel wanted you to go up and . . .

A. Yeah. Bang Joe Peel.

Q. What was your occupation at this time?

A. I was a strong-arm worker.

Q. Do you know whether or not Barney Barnet owned a boat?

A. Yes.

Q. Did you have any conversation with him with reference to that boat?

A. I was in Havana about the end of June. I met Barney and had dinner at his house. He had a boat, twenty-three feet. I said let's get some broads, I mean some girls, at the club and go out on the god damn, I mean boat, and have a ball.

Q. Did you see the boat?

A. Yes.

Q. Were they having it painted then?

A. Yes.

Q. He said he would take you out after it was painted?

A. Yes.

Q. What kind of a boat was that?

A. About a twenty-two, twenty-three footer and it had a little cabin on it.

Mr. Welch pursued the matter no further. His witness was an insolent ruffian with a minimum of credibility, and his testimony did nothing to extricate Judge Peel from the legal pit into which he had fallen. Tedesco had tried to drop a ladder, but it was a fragile thing which would not bear weight. The gentle Welch had about as much control over Tedesco as a drunk flying a jet through a tunnel.

Eugene Spellman conducted the cross-examination. He made it terse and to the point.

Q. Do you know what the punishment is for perjury? [Tedesco rose out of the witness chair, glared up at Judge Smith, who was peering down over the corner of the bench, and looked like an outraged man who will punch the nearest human being.]

A. What are you getting at? You think I would come up here and make a fool out of myself?

Q. You did work for Barney Barnet?

A. Yes.

Q. Where did you work in 1955?

A. At the Harem Club.

Q. Is your full name John Walter Tedesco?

A. Yeah.

Q. Have you ever worked at the Netherlands Cocktail Lounge on Miami Beach?

A. I gave it as a reference once.

Q. Do you swear under oath that you were employed at the Harem Club and you did not begin your employment at the Harem Club on February 8, 1956? [Author's note: This would be after the Chillingworth murders and thus the conversation overheard between Lucky and Barnet would be too late to have any bearing on the plot.]

A. I can't say it like you educated gentlemen. I have to use my own expressions. I don't remember.

Q. You don't remember if you began work on February 8, 1956?

A. No, sir.

Q. How can you remember that you worked at the Harem Club in 1955?

A. I was in and out of that joint—I mean, bar—many times.

The state attorney stood to address the court. "This testimony," O'Connell said, "contains no evidence in this trial."

Judge Smith thought about it a moment, then told Mr. Welch that the proffer of Mr. Tedesco's testimony was denied. The witness was excused, and went through the swinging gate with head lowered, eyes darting animosity at one and all.

It was hardly a good day for Judge Peel. He sat twisting cuticle from his fingernails, listening to witnesses, hoping for some electrifying doubt to be planted in the minds of the jurors. The first witness in the morning established the mood of the day. His name was Robert E. Hawkey and he was a dark, middle-aged man with jug ears and the air of a dozing cobra. He was a radio commentator at a Palm Beach station.

Welch produced some drawings of the area around the Chillingworth home at Manalapan and asked Mr. Hawkey if he drew them. Welch appeared to be startled when Hawkey said: "Maybe you drew them." This was hardly a sympathetic attitude on the part of a defense witness, but Welch moved ahead with his questions as though he didn't know he was about to elicit the wrong answers.

"Didn't you tell me," said Welch, walking up and down and staring at the ceiling, "that if I called you you would come here as a hostile witness?"

The witness said: "Yes, but ask me why."

He turned to the court: "I think Mr. Welch would be a hostile witness too if he was next on Joe Peel's death list. I was told by Henry Lovern that I was next. For years, while this man operated in Palm Beach, I was never more than an arm's length away from a gun. I never even started my car without first lifting the hood."

The witness was withdrawn.

That was the defense opening. It was followed by a serious witness named Emery C. Pickren, who raised bloodhounds in

West Palm Beach. On the morning that the Chillingworths were missing, Pickren, who was a private eye, went home and got his favorite bloodhound, one Holmes, as in Sherlock.

By the time he got back to the beach house, he said, a couple of thousand people were tramping all over the place. He took Holmes into the Chillingworth bedroom and permitted him to sniff some clothes and one closet. The dog pulled on his leash and went sniffing and baying through the living room, out the door, up and down the road, and through the crowd of curious. He had more scents than a bombed-out perfumery.

On the cracked asphalt of an old road in front of the house, Holmes found some parallel skid marks, as though someone had been dragged south toward the highway, but old Holmes sniffed through them and out the other side. Holmes, said Pickren, can work a scent four days old "if there hasn't been too much rain." There were many people. "It would have been a good day to have a peanut concession," the witness said.

Pickren took Holmes home and retired him from criminal sniffing. Holmes is one of the few retired bloodhounds in the country. Today he sniffs trees only, and for fun.

The defense called John Hiatt, who was with the Palm Beach Sheriffs Department at the time of the crime. But he had left word that he didn't feel well, and had left court.

The defense had lots of luck—all bad—throughout the day. Welch put a retired Coast Guardsman on the stand to tell how far it was from the Riviera dock, where Holzapfel claimed he and Bobby Lincoln left in a boat, to the seaside in front of the Chillingworth home. It came out 12.4 miles, but it didn't electrify anybody.

Judge Peel kept staring at his fingers, clasped as in prayer. Fred Leamon took the stand and said he was driving home from a bar in Delray at 10:30 P.M. on June 14, 1955. As he approached within two blocks of the Chillingworth home, he saw a car dart across the road and head south. It was a Mercury or a Ford, he wasn't sure which. It could have been anyone, on any errand not connected with the crime.

At 2.05 P.M. court recessed for the third time because, once more, the defense had no witness ready. At 2:30 P.M. the patience of Judge Smith seemed to have shortened. Welch said he had three witnesses subpoenaed, but none were in court.

"The court," said Judge Smith, "is going to insist that the defense have witnesses here and ready to take the stand at all times."

At 3:05 P.M. the yo-yo jury was ordered back into court and, as they started to enter, Prosecutor O'Connell yelled: "Just a minute. Hold it a minute."

This was the first time that the twelve men and two alternates had been stopped in mid-flight. They were half in, half out of the box.

The defense then told the court that "certain witnesses have been coming to me for the purpose of entrapping me or Mr. Peel." Welch mentioned no names.

However, he put an old, stout man on the stand and he turned out to be C. E. Jones, court stenographer of West Palm Beach. He said there was hardly a crime in Palm Beach within the past forty years that he hadn't taken the shorthand on.

He was in court today to read back the notes he made when the Negro moonshiner, Bobby Lincoln, confessed the Chillingworth murders in Palm Beach court last November. Through the reading, Welch proved that what Lincoln said in court here and what he said last year in Palm Beach were at slight variance.

Judge Peel left the court shaking his head sadly.

139

ELEVENTH
DAY

A young jewel thief sat on the witness stand this morning and yanked the halo off P. O. Wilber, the pious, God-fearing bail bondsman. He and P. O. were good friends and got drunk together. Once, P. O. made a picture of the thief in an intimate situation in a garage apartment and said he only shot the scene to show the crook how easy it was to be framed in Palm Beach.

The thief was Ted Rinehart, the man who was picked up in Texas with a gun which Wilber said was put in Rinehart's luggage by mistake. Mr. Rinehart was as nervous as an old lady knocking on doors on the second floor of a bordello. He didn't know what was going to happen, but he had a feeling it would not be good.

He begged the judge to protect his constitutional rights and he looked at Phil O'Connell the way a canary might glance at

140

a Bengal tiger. Ted was doing a little bit in Raiford Prison. What for doesn't matter. He had chosen thievery as his profession and he was a failure. He had been convicted four times, and if his health held out he might double this number in time.

He told how P. O.—his buddy—made the sexy photo as a sort of joke, but used it later to threaten him into doing the bidding of Mr. Wilber. The bail bondsman, said Rinehart, wanted him to do a "few jobs."

For a half hour, none of this testimony made sense to the spectators because it was not connected with the activities of Judge Joseph A. Peel. The judge was the man on trial here, and the city of Fort Pierce was in a state of restrained hysteria over his guilt or innocence. In the court corridor, young matrons were still selling hot coffee and little cakes, the proceeds of which went to the improvement of Fort Pierce playgrounds for children.

Carlton Welch subpoenaed Ted Rinehart out of Raiford Prison so that the jewel thief could impeach the testimony of P. O. Wilber. However, the witness outdid himself and ended by throwing a new angle into the case. Welch was conducting the interrogation, over the incessant barking of the prosecution, when he appeared to walk into a "solution" of the Chillingworth case which casts doubt on the guilt of his client.

Q. After this photograph was taken did Mr. P. O. Wilber make any threat to you with regard to the use of the photograph?

A. Yes, he did.

Q. What was that threat?

A. I will try to remember his exact words . . . "if you will help me frame Joe Peel, I won't turn this over to the FBI."

Q. Now, during your drinking bouts—excuse me, your honor,

141

for the vernacular—during the occasion of your friendship with Floyd Holzapfel was any other conversation of like effect made?

A. I was never friendly with Floyd Holzapfel.

Q. I beg your pardon, during your friendship with P. O. Wilber, were there any words of like effect?

A. On one or two occasions, he tried to talk me into framing Peel; sometimes he mentioned Holzapfel, sometimes he mentioned them both together, sometimes separate. I can't remember exactly what he told me. I was drunk most of the time.

Welch might have probed a bit further to elicit from the witness why Wilber wanted to frame Judge Peel, or if, in conjunction with the threats, the Chillingworth case was mentioned. He didn't. Mr. Welch permitted the matter to dangle as though he was afraid to pursue it too far.

The cross-examination was undertaken by Phil O'Connell and, in the presence of the jury, he wanted to establish character—or lack of it—at once.

"How many times," the state attorney said, "have you been convicted?" Welch, who had dropped to his chair, popped up at once. He objected. O'Connell addressed the court aggrievedly: "He has already testified he was in jail. I would assume he wasn't there on a pleasure trip." The witness glanced from the prosecutor to the judge. Then he said: "I refuse to answer on the grounds that my testimony may incriminate me."

Judge Smith said that there was nothing incriminating about matters already in the record. The question had nothing to do with pending charges against the witness. Rinehart assumed a betrayed expression: "Are you going to grant me immunity out of anything coming out of this?" he asked.

O'Connell said: "No, sir." The judge ordered Rinehart to answer. Rinehart said: "I still want to know . . ." Welch said:

"I object, your honor . . ." And O'Connell said patronizingly: "Let the judge and me handle this, Mr. Welch." Rinehart listened to the babble of voices and said: "Four."

Q. Four what?

A. Four felonies.

Q. You were not friendly with Mr. Wilber until he got you out on bond on February 25, 1958?

A. Depends on what you mean by friendly.

Q. Were you casual friends or pretty close?

A. Pretty close.

Q. You had no business arrangement?

A. Just the bail bond.

Q. On February twenty-fifth, did you find out he was working with the FBI?

A. I had no proof of it, but I was suspicious.

Q. Did you remain suspicious of it right on through all your dealings with him, that he was working with the police?

A. Well, he did things at certain times that made me less suspicious and sometimes not suspicious at all, and sometimes very suspicious. . . .

Q. At the time Mr. P. O. Wilber talked to you about framing, you say it was Peel one time, Holzapfel the next time, and sometimes together?

A. It wasn't any order.

Q. It was Peel and Holzapfel he was talking about, wasn't it?

A. Yes, sir.

Q. He never told you what he intended to do, did he?

A. No.

Q. He was drunk most of the time, wasn't he? He never told you what he intended to do, did he?

143

A. No.

Animosity between the prosecution and the defense was growing. The judge had taken official cognizance of it several times, and had admonished the gentlemen to be gentlemen. Welch, who was courtly and averse to sarcasm, tried to ignore the snide remarks of the prosecution. O'Connell, who was big and burly and spoke with the snappy growl of a bulldog watching a fly drag his feet across his nose, became impatient with Welch's leisurely manner.

At one time Welch said: "The defense is ready. Is the prosecution ready?" To which O'Connell replied: "We've been ready four and a half years."

One of the minor witnesses of the day was Deputy Sheriff Cecil Sheppard Jr., who sat on the witness stand holding a double-barrel shotgun in a plastic cover. The gun belonged to Judge Peel, and the purpose of introducing it, as a defense exhibit, was to show that Bobby Lincoln was lying, or mistaken, when he said that he used Peel's gun the night of the Chillingworth murders.

Sheppard stood the gun on his thigh. The twin barrels were aimed directly at Judge Smith. The judge flinched and, as he ducked back, the gun revolved slowly on the officer's thigh and followed him. "Mr. Witness," the judge said, "point it up, will you?"

The defense offered the gun as an exhibit. Sheppard left the stand, and handed the gun to Mrs. Joseph A. Peel, who took it and walked to the witness stand. She was a tall, dark, handsome woman—a slender clothes horse with jet wavy hair parted in the middle—and she sat with the gun across her lap.

Judge Smith appeared to be under restraint as he listened to Mrs. Peel identify herself and the gun. She said that she and

144

Joe used this very gun often—in fact, when they were classmates at Stetson University, he had taught her how to hunt with this gun. They had no other double-barrel gun, although they sometimes used a rifle. As Mrs. Peel gained confidence, she began to move the gun around and soon both barrels were magnetized by Judge Smith. They were focused dead on his forehead and, as the barrels waved absentmindedly, his honor tried to set up an opposite rhythm.

Mrs. Peel left the witness stand and handed the gun to Sheriff Jack Norvel, the gentleman rancher who wore brazen orange cowboy shirts with matching shoestring ties. Smith lowered his head and began to make some penciled notes. Norvel tried to break the gun. He couldn't find the catch. This is a source of embarrassment to a sheriff.

Absentmindedly, he handed the gun to Judge Peel. Loaded or unloaded, the defendant now held a double-barrel shotgun in court. Peel braced the stock on his knee, and the gun took dead aim on Judge Smith seven feet away. His honor was still penciling notes. Then he looked up, just in time to stare into both barrels. The end of the gun appeared to be so close that the judge looked as though he was using long black binoculars.

Judge Smith swallowed. Peel broke the gun into three sections and handed them to Norvel. It was nothing, really. Nothing at all.

Welch called George W. Greer to the stand. He was a polygraph expert, who conducted lie detector tests. Mr. Greer testified that he had conducted such a test on a prisoner in Raiford who, as a result, confessed the Chillingworth murders a long time ago. For a moment, there was excitement in the warm court. The state attorney brought out the fact that Greer worked for him and that the man who confessed the murders was certified "to be nuts, your honor." The prisoner was a schizophrenic with paranoid tendencies.

The defense was trying valiantly to toss the murders anywhere but in the small, modest lap of Judge Peel.

Welch asked J. M. Blackburn, a deputy clerk in the Palm Beach court, for the records in a divorce action between Myron Widett, of Chicago and Miami, and Joe Frances Widett, his wife. The case was so hot that Judge Chillingworth, who heard it, ordered the file sealed. It arrived in court sealed and has remained sealed. The object of the defense seemed to be that, in the Widett case, Chillingworth's decision aroused such animosity among the parties to it that they may have been angry enough to kill.

A Coast Guard commander brought records of a small boat sold to Lucky Holzapfel. This puzzled the prosecution, which had maintained that Lucky bought the boat for $450, and used it, with Lincoln, to take the Chillingworths to sea and drown them. The defense attitude had been that if the Chillingworths went by boat, it was someone else's boat. The commander, Charles M. Shepard of Coral Gables, gave testimony as a defense witness which supported the prosecution's contention.

At 5 P.M. the jury was called in so that it could be dismissed for the day. When the jurors got home, their wives would be able to tell them what had been going on in court for the past two weeks.

146

TWELFTH
DAY

The young judge stood this morning, patted the pockets of his jacket, winked over his shoulder at his wife, and walked briskly to the witness stand. Two wire service reporters tiptoed out of court, hurried downstairs and across the street and sent a flash:

"Former Judge Joseph A. Peel Jr. took the stand in his own defense this morning."

It was indeed true. Joe Peel, unimpressed with the defense thus far, had decided to gamble his life against the scorn of his old friend, Phil O'Connell. The young man had spent a restless night. The move he was now making could cost the game, and his life. On the other hand, if he could spin the sweet web of charm which had worked so often on so many

147

strangers, perhaps the jurors would listen and succumb to the bright smile, the sincere eyes; perhaps he could play David against Phil's Goliath; all he had to do was to create a doubt— just a small, persistent doubt.

The judge was so confident, on the witness stand, that he had to feign a little nervousness with his hands to win a sympathetic glance from the jury. Mr. Welch paraded up and down a small space to the left of the witness stand, staring at the ceiling as he intoned his you-all questions. Like a good attorney, he dispensed with the vital question early:

Q. Mr. Peel, I want to ask you if you in any way or at any time did unlawfully contact, hire, procure or command Floyd A. Holzapfel or George David Bobby Lincoln to kill and murder Judge Curtis E. Chillingworth?

A. I did not. Directly or indirectly.

The framing of the question brought a dismal fact to mind: Peel was being tried for the murder of the judge; the matter of Mrs. Chillingworth's life was a separate trial in the event that the young judge skirted the electric chair in this one. The matter of the real estate swindles in and around Melbourne came to about 160 counts of indictment, and there was a prosecutor at this trial whose sole function was to sit in court and make notes of any testimony pertaining to the Insured Capital Corporation. If he were to be tried on all outstanding indictments, Judge Peel could, in poor luck, be sentenced to about 200 years in prison and get two trips to the electric chair.

Welch decided to ask his client for a little background material before proceeding to warmer, and more pertinent, issues. Peel said he graduated from Stetson Law School at Deland in 1949, that he had practiced law, was an elected municipal judge in West Palm Beach for two terms, that he had never been in the habit of riding around Palm Beach with a gun, nor had he ever ridden in an automobile with Floyd Holzapfel and Bobby Lincoln "at the same time."

Peel was strong of voice and wore the long-suffering righteous air of a martyr saint who had changed his mind. He was in a denying mood.

Q. I would like to ask you, sir, if you ever carried on a bolita, gambling or Cuba or any type of operation with Floyd Holzapfel or Bobby Lincoln?

A. No, sir. I did not.

Q. Did you—I withdraw that—Mr. Peel, at the time—I withdraw—I will ask you, sir, did Judge Chillingworth—were you acquainted with Judge Chillingworth?

A. I knew Judge Chillingworth.

Welch spun and skidded on the questions, and O'Connell and Spellman took turns objecting. The defense tried to adduce material about the Shupe divorce case, but couldn't get the decree off the ground. It was the Shupe case which had brought on all of Peel's major troubles. This was the one in which he assured the lady that she had a divorce—or so she maintained—but the truth was that she hadn't. Her mother brought the matter to the attention of Attorney William Cobb of West Palm Beach, and it was filed as a complaint before Judge White. If he found that Peel was in error, it was to be referred to Judge Chillingworth for disciplinary action.

The slender defense attorney tried valiantly to get Peel's story into the record, but the state objected to the form of the questions, their materiality, and charged Mr. Welch with "leading" the witness. The defendant comported himself well. His face, at will, reflected amusement, contrition, puzzlement, righteousness, sincerity and hurt.

The women in the court admired Judge Peel and some of them whispered to others, "I hope nothing happens to him." The witness settled back, leaned forward, rubbed his thumbs together, crossed one leg over the other, looked directly at Phil O'Connell when the prosecutor stood to make objections, and leaned forward with head low, elbows on knees, to think before answering a question. He wore a dark gray suit, a black tie with a little white monogram, a square-edged kerchief and the tented eyebrows of a man who has been hurt.

Peel had an excellent feel for an audience. So had O'Connell, who was reputed to be the best after-dinner speaker in the state of Florida. However, there was a difference. O'Connell led his audience toward his point of view; Peel made his hearers feel that they had discovered a point of view, and that Joe would be abreast of their thinking in a moment or two.

Now and then—not too often to be obvious—the young judge leaned toward the jury of twelve men and two alternates, and made his reply to a question to them. The men in the box leaned toward the witness. One or two nodded with comprehension as Joe spoke.

How did he meet Floyd? Mr. Holzapfel came to Peel with a small claims case in 1952. The judge won a settlement out of court. After that, Lucky became more than a client; he became friendly. "When I was running for my second term as municipal judge, I was a member of American Legion Post 5 in West Palm Beach and I used to sell tickets on fight nights. Floyd came down and used to put vote-for-me cards, with my name on them, on parked cars."

Bobby Lincoln was indicted in Miami on five moonshining counts. Peel took his case and won an acquittal. He went on to a monologue about his troubles as a lawyer, including a reprimand

150

for representing both sides in a divorce action, and the matter of disbarment for giving a woman a decree of divorce which she hadn't won. In this, he faced proceedings by Judge Chillingworth but, when the "big judge" was ready to hear it, he disappeared.

Three months later, Peel said, "Judge Warren, having found me guilty of misconduct and dishonesty, suspended me from the practice of law for ninety days." It wasn't a heavy penalty, but Peel resigned his post as municipal judge of West Palm Beach, and, three years later, he asked the Florida Bar Association for permission to "resign" the practice of law. In May, 1959, he sold his practice and quit law.

Almost all of this was contrary to the testimony of Holzapfel, Lincoln, Jim Yenzer, the undercover agent, and P. O. Wilber, the reformed bail bondsman. There was a lot of lying going on, and the jury was going to have to decide who was doing it.

For example, Floyd and Bobby claimed that, when they got back to the Riviera dock after drowning the Chillingworths, Floyd phoned Peel for fresh shirts and slacks and shoes.

Welch: "On the morning of June 15, 1955, did you deliver any package to Holzapfel or Lincoln?" A. "I did not. On that morning, my wife drove me to my office in the Harvey Building, dropped me off, and . . ."

There was an objection by O'Connell. Welch directed the testimony toward the judge's social relations with Floyd and Bobby Lincoln.

"I never recall going out to dinner with Floyd Holzapfel," Peel said, studying the stains on the old courtroom wall. "I never socialized with him. I had lunch with him two or three or four times. He had coffee with me—let me see—perhaps a dozen times. I went to his house once. Mrs. Holzapfel was there.

151

My reception was such that I never again visited Holzapfel while his wife was present."

This could mean either a very warm welcome or a very cool one.

"Yenzer," the judge continued, "is a cautious man. He asks hypothetical questions. He came to me, for example, and asked me about a man named Floyd and his wife, and a fellow named Barnet, and said they had stolen some radium from a West Palm Beach hospital in 1956 or 1957, and wanted to sell it to a hospital in Cuba . . ."

There was another in an interminable list of objections by O'Connell. At once, Peel switched and said that, after he quit law—or vice versa—he went into the construction business around Lake Worth. In the second week of November, 1958, the Palm Beach newspapers announced that Lew Gene Harvey had floated to the surface of a creek, concrete block and all.

Holzapfel, said the judge, called him. "He made some admissions to me about the matter." At this point, the prosecution hammered so hard at the innocent, inoffensive defense counsel that Carlton Welch announced that he would go to the Florida Supreme Court for a writ of mandamus, to say nothing of certiorari.

The judge hearing this case, D. C. Smith, who was only partly gray when he undertook this assignment, ran his hand through his snow-white hair and said that nobody was going anywhere for any purpose. All hands would stay here and proceed with the case.

O'Connell, who can voice more than a terse objection, said that Peel had come to his office one day and cried into a handkerchief and begged for immunity in the Lew Gene Harvey case, and the Chillingworth case, in the presence of three witnesses. The jury was out but the press was in. In return, Peel promised to tell all about those mysteries. O'Connell was, in effect, testifying to the press. The prosecutor seldom surrendered an opportunity to toss a barb at Peel, even when the words were shaded with impropriety.

A few minutes later, when Joe Peel was telling how he felt a growing fear toward Floyd Holzapfel, Phil O'Connell jumped up to say: "He ought to be afraid of Holzapfel. He paid eighteen hundred dollars to have him killed." This was accompanied by a knowing look around the court.

The so-called "growing fear" experienced by the defendant was shared, it seems, by some of the other characters. Peel was afraid of Holzapfel; Floyd was afraid of Peel; Bobby Lincoln was afraid that both would beat him to confession and immunity; Yenzer and Wilber played a dangerous double game and were afraid they wouldn't get the reward; O'Connell was afraid that, after waiting five long years to get Peel, he might miss; Holzapfel was afraid that, while he was hiding in South America, Judge Peel might be friendly with Mrs. Holzapfel; Welch was afraid of the vituperation of his client; Judge Smith was afraid that the trial would never get in motion.

The witness claimed that to incur Floyd's anger was a dangerous thing. "Jim Yenzer was in fear of his life. He and Floyd were caught stealing guns in Miami and they agreed to split the cost of defense. Jim got away from the police, but Floyd was caught. Now Lucky claimed that Jim owed nineteen hundred dollars of the defense bill. Yenzer was afraid . . .

"Floyd asked me to go into an eight per cent loan business. I said no. He persisted. His friends offered to come in on a building business in Orlando at eight per cent. I said okay. Floyd was dangerous. One day he phoned and all he said was that he had a friend who had a little girl [Peel had a daughter, as well as a son] and the little girl was killed because her father talked too much. He made a special point of telling me this story."

The young judge's burgeoning nervousness about his friend Floyd grew alarmingly when Yenzer, in October 1959, said to Peel: "Joe, you know you're a threat to Floyd as long as you're walking around." In the same month, Henry Lovern of the Sheriffs Bureau called on Peel twice to ask where Holzapfel might be. Peel claims that his fear grew to hysteria.

It was at that time that Peel decided to have Lucky killed. He worked out a plan, as usual, to have someone else do the work and he thought, as usual, that a disappearance, preferably at sea, would be the best means of ringing the curtain down on Floyd. Peel's weakness was that he needed someone as a sounding board for ideas—even unlawful ones. So he talked it over with Donald Miles, his partner in the building business. This is akin to Frankenstein discussing his plans with Shirley Temple.

Miles became "very upset" and went along with Joe's plan to hire someone—preferably Jim Yenzer—to do the work. For a time it seemed that several of these people were thinking seriously of killing several others. The young judge was aware of Holzapfel's jealousy of his wife, but Peel, who said that after one meeting with Mrs. Holzapfel he would not visit Lucky's house again, changed his mind when Floyd went to South America.

"Mrs. Holzapfel called me after her husband left for South America and asked me if she could meet me in New York for a couple of days before she rejoined Floyd. I did. I discussed with her the Harvey case and the Chillingworth case. Later, she called me from Rio—in all, three times. She returned to the United States and, in July of 1960, I met her in Miami. In fact, I know where she is right now."

This was a mysterious piece of testimony because counsel never asked the obvious question: "Why did you go all the way to New York to discuss two murder cases with Mrs. Holzapfel? What did she know about them? What did you know?"

When Mrs. Holzapfel returned from South America, she went to South Carolina, where she stayed with her parents. She phoned Peel and added to his fear of Floyd. "She told me that Floyd just phoned from South America. He accused her of improper relations with me. Twenty minutes later, Holzapfel called me. He was very upset. He said he had heard from P. O. Wilber that I had been staying at a motel in Orlando with his wife. I said it wasn't true. I wasn't there. He called me a liar. He said he had also heard that Mrs. Holzapfel was running around with a couple of salesmen, and he knew all about it.

"I told him I knew nothing about it. Floyd said she was running around with a shoe salesman. I said the truth was that she had only gone bowling with a shoe salesman."

Welch cut in: "Have you ever had improper relations with Mrs. Holzapfel?" A. I . . . have . . . not.

The defense now moved toward the close of its direct examination, and asked some questions about Peel's travels just before his arrest in the autumn of 1960.

Q. Why did you leave Atlanta for Eau Gallie?

A. Don Miles phoned me. He told me that Holzapfel was in Eau Gallie looking for me like a raving maniac. Don wanted to kill him. I told him, "Don, don't do it. I'll come down there." I hired a private plane, I got a gun and flew out that very evening . . .

Q. Did you, prior to that time, have a visa permit to leave the country if you wanted to?

A. You mean a passport?

155

Q. Yes.

A. Yes.

Q. Would you tell us why you flew back to Eau Gallie where Mr. Holzapfel was?

A. My wife and children . . .

Q. What are the ages of your children?

A. We have a girl, nine, and a boy, five.

Q. I will ask you where you spent the night on your arrival there?

A. As soon as Miles said that Floyd was back, I phoned my wife. I told her to take the children to my brother's house. I picked them up there and we all spent the night at Don's house.

Q. Immediately after September thirtieth, 1960, what did you, Mr. Miles, and your families do?

A. Went to Daytona Beach.

Q. Did you take your wife and family?

A. Yes, sir.

Q. Did Mr. Miles take his wife and family?

A. Yes, sir. All three of them.

Q. Mr. Peel, on the thirtieth day of September in Room 127 of the Holiday Motel in Melbourne, did you say to Jim Yenzer, when he attempted to ask you something about the Chillingworth case, or as he called it the C case, "No, no. That is something you just don't talk about"?

A. Yes, sir. I did.

Q. Were you placed under arrest at a subsequent date to September thirtieth?

A. Yes.

Q. When was this?

A. On November, I believe it was the fifth, in Chattanooga, Tennessee.

156

Q. I am speaking about prior to September thirtieth. Were you?

A. Yes, on a charge of conspiracy to kill Holzapfel.

Q. Did you leave Florida?

A. Yes, I left on October fifth, 1960.

Q. Did you at that time take your passport with you?

A. No. I did not. I left my passport with my wife at our house in Eau Gallie.

Q. Did you when you were out of the state keep in touch with Don Miles?

A. Not constantly, but for the month of October I talked to him four or five times.

Q. Did he then entice you down to the . . .

Mr. O'Connell objected to the word "entice." He was sustained and, as usual, Mr. Welch switched the line of questioning at once.

Q. Did you pursue your conversation with Miles at the Patton Hotel in Chattanooga?

A. Yes, I did.

Q. While you were at the Patton Hotel, will you tell us what Mr. Miles did and what was the conversation between you all, and I will ask you this: did you know that Mr. Miles was co-operating with the police?

A. No.

Q. Did you think he was your friend?

A. I certainly did.

Q. What did you do when you went to Chattanooga?

A. When I got to Chattanooga he asked me to come on by. I went right up to see him in the room even before I checked in. He had a bottle of liquor, just the kind I always drink, and some ginger ale. We talked.

Q. Did he make any special discussion about the Chillingworth case?

A. Yes. I didn't realize he was pumping me. He said: "You know, Joe . . ."

O'Connell was spending most of his time on his feet and he was quick to object that this line was immaterial and irrelevant. Judge Smith agreed.

Q. When you were arrested in Chattanooga, did you resist returning to Florida?

A. No, sir. I promptly waived extradition. When I walked out of the room, I never saw so many police officers in my life. They took me to jail and asked me if I wanted to waive extradition on the . . .

The state attorney interjected that this was improper testimony. Welch argued with the prosecutor, and Judge Smith rapped for order. O'Connell asked if Welch was testifying, or Peel. Welch said to the prosecutor: "You have done quite a bit of testifying yourself, Mr. O'Connell." The state attorney turned on his fighter's grin and said: "Don't mimic me, Mr. Welch."

Q. Do you recall the date that you were transported from the West Palm Beach County jail to the county jail of Fort Pierce?

A. Around the eighteenth of December, I think.

Q. Prior to that time had Bobby Lincoln testified in a proceeding against you and been granted immunity for testimony against you in West Palm Beach?

A. Yes, sir, he has testified in a preliminary hearing in the Chillingworth case.

Q. In your presence?

A. Oh yes, absolutely.

Q. I want to ask you, Mr. Peel, did you give . . . Did you at any time in West Palm Beach, Florida, give this boy, Johnson, who testified before us here, slip him any poison to be given to Floyd Holzapfel?

A. I did not and I want an opportunity to explain what happened.

Judge Smith nodded that he might proceed with the explanation.

A. When I was brought back to West Palm Beach my being brought back was publicized and I was put in a maximum security cell for two or three days, at which time the jailer transferred me to another maximum security cell behind three locked doors. I was opposed to being transferred in there, because there were three other fellows in there and I knew what can happen when you get . . . [Objection by the state was sustained. The witness was instructed to answer more directly.]

A. No, I didn't give it to him. I was confined in cell number 305. I was never allowed to return from downstairs without being guarded. In the cell I wasn't allowed to have any cigarettes, coat hangers, anything metal or anything like that.

At 4:30 P.M. Welch said he had no further questions. It was the weirdest, most complicated murder story of the century. Tomorrow, the state attorney would have a chance to smooth it out.

THIRTEENTH
DAY

The witness arrived in court looking like the star at a shotgun wedding. He wore a charcoal gray silk suit, a bright tie, a big smile, and he was surrounded by deputy sheriffs. Judge Peel's ebullience was directed to friends sitting in the courtroom pews, to his counsel, his wife Imogene, who blew a kiss, and Jack Norvel, the sheriff. When Judge Smith entered the courtroom and swept up to the bench, Peel listened to the "Hear ye, hear ye" of the bailiff, and stood facing the jury box.

He was asked to sit in the witness box and the smile lingered until he settled himself and faced the state attorney. Mr. O'Connell addressed himself to the court and said he wanted to read a transcript of some recording tapes picked up by Agent Lovern at the Holiday Inn when Peel and Yenzer and Donald Miles were plotting the murder of Holzapfel. He was sorry, he said, that some of the language was foul, but it would have to be read in open court.

Judge Smith made a grave announcement to the spectators warning everyone that some of the language in the dialogue was bound to be disgusting to human ears—especially ladylike ears —and for those who had sensibilities, there was time to leave court now. No one left. The ladies inched forward on their seats; some of the little ones leaned back against matronly bosoms and stuck thumbs in their mouths.

Some of the words quoted from the mouth of Peel were a bit too virile and gamy, but O'Connell wrung an admission from the witness that the transcript was faithful to the original conversation. In essence, the transcript reported:

Peel saying that P. O. Wilber was the one who sent Floyd the money to get back from Rio. Holzapfel wanted $30,000 from Peel and Insured Capital Corporation, and said he needed half of it to pay debts. Jim Yenzer, presumably, was about to go out and kill Floyd. Peel told him: "Now, Jim. This is a big deal. We have talked about it before. He has a wallet in his coat, a big folding wallet. In that is an eight-page letter with complete details of Insured Capital Corporation finances. We have got to get that letter and photostats of four or five canceled checks."

Peel gave Yenzer $3,000 and promised that $2,000 more would be mailed to him in Miami. The young judge said he was going to check out of this motel, and "When we hear that the job has been done, we will drive to Tennessee. You will have your money Monday or Tuesday of next week."

It was obvious that Joe did not want Yenzer to talk to Floyd before killing him. "He'll kill you, Jim," he said. "You can't talk to that man." Peel mentioned the papers in the wallet again and warned: "He is going to pry the lid off and put a noose around our necks." Peel and Miles produced pistols and gave Yenzer his choice.

The witness, of course, was not currently on trial for trying to kill his old friend. There was a charge of attempted murder against the judge, but it could wait.* O'Connell was about to try for an admission of guilt from Peel. The state attorney had a note from Peel, written immediately after his arrest on October 4, 1960.

Q. I have here, Mr. Peel, a letter and ask you if you have ever seen it before?

A. Yes, sir. I have.

Q. Whose handwriting is it in?

A. That is in mine, Mr. O'Connell.

Q. Did you write this letter?

A. Yes, sir. I did.

Q. On October fourth, 1960?

A. Yes, sir.

The letter was offered in evidence and admitted as State Exhibit 42. O'Connell received permission to read the note. In substance, it said: This is to certify that on this day after being interrogated at the Holiday Inn Motel, I request permission to talk to State Attorney Phil O'Connell of West Palm Beach, Florida. I am being transported voluntarily to West Palm Beach. I have not been put under arrest and have been treated with courtesy and respect.

The introduction of the letter brought up a procedural point, and that was that all defendants should be aware of everything

*Peel was tried later on this charge, and acquitted.

162

the state might introduce as evidence, and be prepared to counteract it. O'Connell, obviously, was going to use the letter to show that Joe Peel was so frightened after his arrest that he wanted to see Phil at once to ask for immunity in return for helping to put Holzapfel and Lincoln in the electric chair. No one as law-wise as Peel would be caught without an explanation —a palatable, credible explanation—for this letter and all other evidence in O'Connell's hands.

Q. After you signed this letter, did you come to West Palm Beach?

A. Yes, sir.

Q. Did you come to talk to the state attorney in the county courthouse?

A. Yes, sir. I was accompanied there by Henry Lovern, Ross Anderson and, I believe, John Kirk, Jr.

The two antagonists, at this point, settled into permanent attitudes. Phil O'Connell made a small attempt to hide his scorn of Peel. He snapped his questions in a low growl and permitted venom to remain in his glance and on his lips. Peel looked up at O'Connell out of the tops of his eyes, a small, naïve boy who, in bewildered innocence, did not quite understand what the prosecutor was driving at.

Q. At that time, did you state that you would tell about the Chillingworth case if you were granted immunity for any participation you may have had in it?

A. Mr. O'Connell, if I had tried to talk to you about immunity in the Chillingworth case, you should have arrested me that night.

Q. You didn't state to me that if you were granted immunity, you would tell about the Chillingworth case?

A. No, sir. I did not.

Q. Was it discussed with you that night?

A. Yes, sir. It was.

Q. Did you refuse to make any statement about it?

A. I do not recall.

Q. Did you discuss with me immunity about the Harvey case?

A. Yes, sir.

Q. Did you then request immunity for any participation you may have had in the Harvey case?

A. No, sir. Not in those words. I talked to you and told you what the Florida Sheriffs Bureau had done to me in this account. They had questioned me in the plan to kill Floyd Holzapfel. I told you I was shocked at what they had done to me. I was living in Brevard County. They had surreptitiously sent in James Yenzer and after months and months of his badgering me I became so very upset I entered into a plot to kill Holzapfel.

I told you I didn't think that type of law enforcement was right, fair, proper or legal. I told you about the Florida Sheriffs Bureau having come to see me prior to November and December. They had threatened that they would see that I was filed as an accessory before the fact in the Harvey case if I didn't disclose what I had been told by Holzapfel concerning the crime. I wrote to my lawyer. I was told not to disclose any information and that I could not be made an accessory before the fact . . . They told me I would be charged then as an accessory after the fact.

Q. You thought you would be charged as an accessory after the fact?

A. I told you they had threatened me if I did not disclose Holzapfel's conversation with me, that they would see that I was so charged. I asked you: "Phil, in your opinion do you think I could be charged in the Harvey case?" You told me you didn't think I could be charged with anything, that you didn't think I had anything to do with it.

Q. Didn't you go out and call another lawyer that night and make the statement: "Sometimes you lose. In this case [Chillingworth] I have lost." Not once, but time and time again. Did you use those words?

A. No, sir. I told you in effect . . .

The prosecutor was becoming nettled. The witness was transposing statements and slightly altering others to make himself look like an innocent victim of persecution. O'Connell stopped growling. He shouted.

Q. Did you ever use those words?

A. No, sir. I didn't.

Q. You didn't say: "Sometimes you win. Sometimes you lose. In this case I have lost"?

A. I can't give you the words I did use. I told you I had committed moral wrong in Brevard County.

Q. Didn't you go outside to call a lawyer and repeat to him about immunity in the Chillingworth case and talk to him about it? [The witness began to falter, ever so slightly. He wasn't certain whether O'Connell could produce the lawyer as a rebuttal witness.]

A. I did talk to him about immunity, but I cannot recall its being in regard to the Chillingworth case. Mr. Anderson, before he took me to West Palm Beach, first of all told me he had an instanta subpoena from the state attorney with regard to questioning me about the Chillingworth case. I talked to the lawyer and talked to him about the Harvey case and I told him Anderson had told me he had an instanta subpoena from you to take me back to West Palm Beach to be questioned about the Chillingworth case . . .

165

Two rows of benches inside the court enclosure had been reserved for visiting lawyers and jurists. They were full. The attorneys wanted to see this fight between two well-known lawyers, two former friends who were locked in a deadly struggle in which but one could win. There was some feeling among them that O'Connell had sufficient evidence before the jury to hang Joe Peel, and that any lengthy cross-examination would help the defendant, not the prosecutor.

At one point, a question by the state attorney caused Peel to laugh. "Don't laugh," O'Connell said sternly, "this is a murder trial." The witness stopped, shook his head sadly, and said: "No one knows that better than I, Mr. O'Connell." The prosecutor read from the tapes the plot to kill Floyd Holzapfel and kept interrupting himself to ask: "Did you say that? Are these your words?" The young judge said yes, they were. O'Connell spent more time unraveling the Holzapfel attempted murder and the Harvey moonshine killing than he did on the Chillingworth case.

His cross-examination, which was expected to require at least one day, perhaps two, died in negation after two hours and forty minutes.

Q. In the Chillingworth case, did you ask for immunity?

A. No, sir. If I did, you would have arrested me right there and then.

Q. Did you or did you not ask for immunity in the Chillingworth case?

A. No, sir.

O'Connell tossed a sheaf of papers onto the plain desk before him. "No more questions," he said. Welch stood for redirect examination and tried to exonerate his client from the crime of attempted murder on Floyd Holzapfel.

Q. On the thirtieth day of September 1960, had you by that time been accused personally by Holzapfel and informed by Holzapfel that Jim Wilber had written to him stating that you had been sleeping with his wife?

A. Yes, sir. He had called me from Rio on the fifteenth of December and, in the course of that conversation, he accused me of matters along those lines.

Q. In the conversation with Yenzer, did you expect Holzapfel to come up shooting?

A. I certainly did.

Q. Did you think that's what his method of operation would be?

A. I certainly did.

Q. Other than Mr. Miles' feeling about who Holzapfel was out to get, who were you afraid he was going to get?

A. The very reason that I came back was for that. I was very much frightened that my daughter was in danger, and I wanted to make sure that my family was removed from any danger.

O'Connell sniffed an atomizer. Judge Smith looked up in surprise. He said he thought that the state planned to keep the defendant on the stand all day. The state attorney remained seated. "I thought so too," he said.

Court recessed early because the defense could not find sufficient witnesses around the court to keep the trial in motion. The court had viewed, with growing impatience, the haphazard manner in which the defense assembled its witnesses. Mr. Welch sometimes appeared to be plotting his case the evening before each session. He spent some of the night hours in a local law office, over a motion picture theater, and sometimes he did not get back to his motel room, leaning slightly against the weight of a heavy briefcase, until the late hours.

When court recessed at lunchtime today, the reporters filed their stories and sat over coffee discussing the cross-examination of Peel. All admitted that the high spot of this trial was a disappointment. One figured that, of the 150 minutes O'Connell had Peel on the witness stand, only four were devoted to questions about the Chillingworth murders, and those were repetitious.

All agreed that O'Connell was too smart a prosecutor to permit Joe Peel to get off the stand unscathed. Still, this was what happened. Peel looked like a happy, exultant man as he walked out of court that day. He had not been hammered mercilessly and, if it was part of the prosecution strategy to hang Peel on the testimony of such as Holzapfel and Lincoln, then it became understandable. No one could comprehend why the state prosecutor, to whom this case was a personal matter, waited over five years to ask a few questions about immunity, and quit.

There must have been more to it than that.

FOURTEENTH
DAY

Court opened with Judge Smith displaying increasing concern about the length of the trial. He reminded counsel that he had asked before that they please have their witnesses ready. Judge Smith's motive was not merely the court's time; he had fourteen men in the jury box who were living in isolation at the height of the Florida season. The judge and Mr. O'Connell were openly solicitous of these twelve men and two alternatives, and no one wanted to irritate them.

The defense, said the judge, had been advised to have all its remaining witnesses on hand in the witness room, and the state had been requested to have its rebuttal witnesses ready. Smith said that he had been thinking of holding night sessions to speed

169

the conclusion of the case. Mr. Welch said that he had a new witness, from Jacksonville, but as he had not heard about him until two days ago, it might require time for him to get to Fort Pierce.

Judge Smith said that it was time to get all defense witnesses on planes for Fort Pierce; the trial would have to proceed. Welch then asked permission to play part of the state's tapes to impeach the testimony of Floyd Holzapfel. O'Connell got to his feet and said no, play all the tapes or none. This would take four days of squeaky listening. Mr. Welch dropped the thought and called P. O. Wilber as a witness with a proffer. The jury was excused once more and, when Welch failed to adduce the type of testimony he wanted from the bail bondsman, Wilber was excused.

Welch called a lawyer, Frank Maynard, as a witness. Mr. Maynard was the man in Joe Peel's office when Edna Trepp, waiting to go to lunch, overheard Peel say that he got Chillingworth and now he would have to get O'Connell.

Q. Did Mr. Peel, ever in your presence, make the statement "We got Judge Chillingworth . . ." and it was, shall we say, in a laughing way, you know, hah hah hah, but then when he came to Mr. Phil O'Connell's statement he became very serious and in dead earnest said: "Now we got to get Phil O'Connell"? Maynard, a middle-aged attorney with gray hair, asked Mr. Welch to repeat the question. The defense attorney shortened it.

A. He did not.

When the state attorney stood to question Mr. Maynard, the witness began to bristle. The dialogue was slow at the start, then moved at an accelerated pace until the interrogations and the answers came so fast that the court reporter had difficulty trying to follow it.

Q. At the conclusion of your statement, when you walked out of my door, didn't you come back and voluntarily say that you had gone to Miami with Joe Peel and on the way to Miami, didn't you say you said something to him about the Chillingworth case and Joe said to you: "Anybody who knows anything about the Chillingworth case doesn't live"?

Maynard said he remembered a conversation with Peel, but didn't think that those were the exact words.

The defense appeared to be stunned. Peel stared at the man who had come to court to be his witness, and the young judge's mouth hung open. Mr. Welch listened in amazement. Some of the spectators wondered why, if Maynard had such a conversation with O'Connell, he did not tell it to Welch before taking the witness stand. His testimony impeaching Edna Trepp could not match the weight of the admission he was about to make.

Q. Why did you discuss the Chillingworth case with him?

A. We were just talking. I discussed the case with many people. I discussed it with you, Mr. O'Connell . . .

Q. Did you say he scared you and you would never mention it to him again?

A. No, sir.

Q. What did you say?

A. I didn't make that statement to you or to anyone else. I made no such statement like that— "I was scared."

Q. Let me ask you again: what did you say?

A. I asked Mr. Peel about it and he made some statement to the effect "I believe if anyone knew who killed the Chillingworths, he wouldn't be alive" or words to that effect.

Q. When you asked him, riding to Miami after the Chillingworth deaths, he said anybody who . . .

Mr. Welch interrupted to say: "After the Chillingworth case?"

171

O'Connell became angry and turned to Welch and said loudly and laconically: "After the Chillingworth deaths, deaths, murders, deaths, deaths. . . ." Welch said he objected to this. Judge Smith overruled the motion.

Q. Weren't those exact words used by you? You voluntarily came back after you went out—when you asked Joe Peel about the Chillingworth case on the way to Miami he turned to you and said "Anybody who knows about the Chillingworth case doesn't live." Did you or did you not make that exact statement?

A. I did not.

O'Connell sat. Mr. Welch now had a choice. He could open the new vein of information, or he could seal it by excusing the witness. It seemed to be a dangerous matter to pursue, but Mr. Welch decided to ask the fateful question.

Q. Could I ask you, sir, what he did say?

A. At the conclusion of the interrogation that was transcribed, of which I have a copy here, and before I had gone out of the room, I did say to Mr. O'Connell that I had gone to Miami with Mr. Peel and during the course of the ride I had asked him, in effect, about the Chillingworth case, or we were discussing it and he said in his opinion, "anyone who knew anything about that case, their lives wouldn't be worth a plugged nickel" or words like that.

Mr. Welch sat. He didn't count on O'Connell, who stood.

Q. Didn't you say you got so upset that you would never mention it to him again?

A. No, sir.

Q. Didn't you say from the beginning you suspected Joe in the Chillingworth case?

A. No, I said I was suspicious of Joe, as were a lot of people. Welch began to look like a man who was trying to run fast on crutches. He had lots of ideas, lots of witnesses, but almost everything that was asked seemed to be objectionable to the state or to the court. Judge Smith said: "I'm not going to permit this line of questioning"; O'Connell said: "Why must he get another ruling when he's already had four on the same subject?" The witnesses came and went. They wanted to testify to conversations which, by innuendo, might make it appear that persons other than Judge Peel had a motive for killing the Chillingworths, or they were there to impeach Holzapfel or Yenzer.

The defense proffered testimony beyond the ears of the jury, and this too was spurned by the court. Faster and faster moved Mr. Welch, but he was a man on a treadmill before a moving screen. He had no speed; only the illusion. Late in the morning he made a proffer of evidence. When it too was denied, he began to rummage through a sheaf of papers. Welch took so much time that lawyers began to wander around the enclosure of the court, whispering and smiling and renewing old acquaintances.

The judge watched, still clutching his patience in both hands. At last he said: "Do you have anything further to state, Mr. Welch?" Welch said mysteriously: "The record will speak for itself." Judge Smith seemed unable to comprehend. Welch kept reading the papers. "Suppose, sir," the judge said, "since it is nearing lunch hour, that during the noon hour you might analyze the files and the court will convene after lunch. Is that satisfactory?"

It was. Court recessed and Judge Peel was taken back to his cell shaking his head and trying to smile for the newsreel and television cameramen waiting down on the lawn. After lunch, Judge Smith, looking well fed and at peace with the world, ordered the defense to continue. Welch made a few proffers, and then said he had a witness who could be expected at 5 P.M.

173

Judge Smith lost his temper for the first time. "Gentlemen," he said, "this trial is continuing." His voice became louder. "The court is ready to hear your next witness. Call him." Welch called Sidney J. Catts, Jr.

The judge was not mollified. "Again," he said, "I wish associate counsel to go out and get on the telephone and any witnesses who are not here, tell them to get on an airplane and head for Fort Pierce immediately. This trial is going to continue."

Attorney Catts took the stand. He was an elderly man with neatly shaved jowls and the air of an impeccable businessman. Mr. Welch nodded to him and said: "Before the jury is called, my client has authorized me to release Mr. Catts from any attorney-client privilege." O'Connell snapped: "We understood there wasn't any."

Catts was the man on whom Peel called for advice the night he and O'Connell discussed immunity in West Palm Beach. The nub of his testimony was:

". . . sometime around ten o'clock at night I was awakened by a deputy sheriff. He told me that Mr. Peel was at the courthouse with Phil O'Connell and he wanted me to call. I couldn't call Mr. O'Connell because the switchboard was off. I told him to have Mr. Peel call me, so he did.

"When they called, Mr. O'Connell was on the phone. He told me that Joe Peel was there in his office and wanted to talk to me. He said he was there under investigation in the Harvey case, not the Chillingworth case. He said he had offered Joe Peel immunity in the Harvey case, not in the Chillingworth case, if Joe Peel would tell him what he knew about the murder.

"I told Phil, Mr. O'Connell, that I couldn't converse with Mr. Peel or advise anybody because I represented the sheriff of Palm Beach County and I had talked to him on many occasions about Joe Peel and the Harvey case, and during the summer I had

174

talked to Henry Lovern of the Sheriffs Bureau about the case. I said I couldn't advise Mr. Peel about the Harvey case.

"Mr. O'Connell said: 'Well, if Peel wants to talk to you, talk to him anyway.' So Joe Peel got on the phone. Peel said he was there with O'Connell and O'Connell offered him immunity in the Harvey case if he would tell what he knew about it, and asked me what to do about it. I told him, 'Joe, I can't represent you because I represent the sheriff of Palm Beach County.' I said I wouldn't be qualified to represent him."

If one can form a conclusion from what is on the record, Judge Peel was not a party to the Harvey murder. It was executed by Floyd Holzapfel and Bobby Lincoln in retaliation for what they thought were tipoffs to the police about moonshine establishments by Lew Gene Harvey of Jacksonville. If Peel had any knowledge of the crime, it probably came from Floyd. Even at that, it might be privileged knowledge because Holzapfel told Peel the story as a client tells a lawyer.

Welch asked: Did Mr. Peel ever say to you that he had requested immunity?

A. No, sir.

Q. What did you tell him?

A. I told him: "Joe, you know law as well as I do. Get yourself another lawyer." He said: "Who?" I said, "I don't know. I can't represent you." He said: "Who do you recommend?" I said, "I can't recommend anyone." Then O'Connell came back on the phone and said: "Sid, tell him what you would do. Not as an attorney, but what you would do yourself." I told him again I couldn't tell him what to do because I represented the sheriff.

O'Connell could not shake the witness's story that Peel and O'Connell talked about the Harvey murder on that night, and not the Chillingworth case. It looked like a solid little victory for Peel—not enough to exonerate him, but sufficient to make the jury feel that the methods of O'Connell and the Sheriffs Bureau were devious and far from honorable. O'Connell's answer to this was: "You don't go skunk huntin' in a tuxedo."

A half hour after Catts left the stand, the defense rested its case, subject to the call of one witness who would testify about phone calls to South America. The state elected to call its rebuttal witnesses and, until the first one began to testify, no one in court except O'Connell and Eugene Spellman knew that a time bomb had been ticking under Judge Peel for weeks.

The witness was Ross Anderson, assistant state director of the Florida Sheriffs Bureau. Mr. Anderson was a dark, handsome, fortyish man who spoke softly, laughed easily, and knew his business. He was on the witness stand to testify to a trick which can only be described as questionable. Eugene Spellman led him through identification down to October 4, 1960, when Joe Peel was apprehended and asked to be taken to Phil O'Connell for a talk.

Q. After you arrived in Palm Beach did you have occasion to overhear any conversation between Mr. O'Connell and Joseph Peel?

A. Yes.

Q. What occasion was that and where were you?

A. I was in a room adjacent to the grand jury room in the courthouse.

Peel, in court, covered his eyes with his hand. Under it, he kept shaking his head no. He could not believe that he had been betrayed under a flag of truce. He had gone to O'Connell to bargain, and the state attorney had posted Ross Anderson in the next room as an eavesdropper. The young judge, certain that he was alone with his tormentor, probably spoke freely.

Q. Did you observe Joseph Peel?

A. I could not see him.

Q. Do you know the voice of Joseph Peel?

A. Yes. I had had conversations with him intermittently through the day.

Q. Would you state what recollection you have of the conversation between Mr. O'Connell and Mr. Peel relating to the Chillingworth case?

A. Mr. Peel discussed with Mr. O'Connell several things, including the Chillingworth case. In the Chillingworth case, he requested immunity for his testimony.

Q. You overheard the conversation relating to him regarding immunity?

A. Joe Peel told Mr. O'Connell that he was in a lot of trouble and outlined the three cases in which he was involved. Then the question of immunity in the Chillingworth case came up.

Q. What response did Mr. O'Connell make?

A. Mr. O'Connell flatly refused.

Q. Did he make any other statement?

A. Mr. O'Connell said he would give him immunity in another case.

Q. Did Mr. O'Connell ever state to Mr. Peel that if he was not involved in the Chillingworth case why did he want immunity?

A. Several times.

Q. Did Joe Peel know that you were present there?

A. No, sir.

Mr. Spellman limped back to his chair at the counsel table. He nodded to Welch, who stood forlornly like a man who has climbed a long, long way, and who finds the mountain growing above him.

Q. Did you have any occasion to hear Joe Peel go to the telephone?

A. Yes.

177

Q. Did you overhear that conversation?

A. Portions of it, if not all of it.

Q. Did you hear him ask for any immunity in that conversation?

A. To the best of my knowledge, no.

Q. How long did Joe Peel stay there in the grand jury room with Mr. O'Connell?

A. He stayed approximately thirty to forty minutes with Mr. O'Connell, following which he asked for an opportunity to call an attorney. There was a great deal of difficulty getting in touch with his attorney.

Q. Was John Kirk [sheriff] with you?

A. Yes.

Q. And he didn't make any arrest?

A. No.

Q. You were present in the Room 129, I believe, from September thirtieth to October third, were you not? [Objection by the state. Overruled by Judge Smith.]

A. Would you rephrase that question, sir?

Q. As of October fourth, you had been present with Henry Lovern in Room 129 of the Holiday Motel in Melbourne, had you not?

A. Yes.

Q. May I ask what warrant you had for Joe Peel then?

A. A warrant for conspiracy to murder Floyd Holzapfel.

Mr. Welch said he had no more questions. Ross Anderson left the witness stand and Phil O'Connell called Henry Lovern, Anderson's Lil' Abner assistant. The nets and traps, so carefully set up to catch the young judge, and nobody but the young judge, continued to fall into place.

Lovern was questioned by Assistant State Attorney Charles

F. Brown. Brown had gray hair in tight curls and he spoke in a confessional whisper.

Q. Did you know Jim Yenzer?

A. Yes.

Q. Did Mr. Yenzer ever work for the Florida Sheriffs Bureau?

A. He had a contractual arrangement with the Florida Sheriffs Bureau.

Q. When was your first contact with Mr. Yenzer?

A. My first contact was February 1959.

Q. Was he participating in this case?

A. Yes, he was . . .

Q. Were you present on November fourteenth, 1960 in the grand jury room of the Palm Beach County courthouse?

A. Yes.

Q. Did you hear any conversation that took place between Mr. Maynard and Mr. O'Connell at that time?

A. Yes.

Q. Would you relate to the jury what you heard?

A. Mr. Maynard had previously given testimony to Mr. O'Connell in my presence. After his testimony was completed, Mr. Maynard left the room. I remained with Mr. O'Connell. Maynard then returned and told us that he had previously taken a trip with Joe Peel to Miami. During this trip he said: "I asked Joe Peel about the Chillingworth case." He said Joe Peel turned his head around to him—[Objection by Mr. Welch. Overruled by Judge Smith.]—immediately stating: "That is one if you know too much about, or talk too much about, you don't live." Maynard then said: "Needless to say, I got scared and didn't ask any more questions."

That tended to impeach Attorney Maynard's testimony, and now Assistant Prosecutor Brown moved on to the big kill—to get Lovern to support what Ross Anderson had already said about the private conversation between O'Connell and Peel on October 4, 1960.

Q. Did you overhear the conversation between Joe Peel and Mr. O'Connell?

A. Yes.

Q. Would you relate it to the jury?

A. I was immediately adjacent to the grand jury room in a small office. The door had a half-inch space at the bottom. I laid down on the floor with my ear next to that space. I could hear Joe Peel say: "Phil, they got me. They got me cold. Sometimes you win. Sometimes you lose. This time I lost. I have got to have immunity." [He was talking about the Holzapfel plot.]

Mr. O'Connell told him that he did not have jurisdiction in a matter in Brevard County and he could not talk about it. Mr. O'Connell said that he understood that Joe Peel knew something about the Chillingworth case. Joe Peel said: "I have got to have immunity. I have got to have immunity. I have got to have immunity."

Q. Did he make those statements after Mr. O'Connell asked him about the Chillingworth case?

A. Immediately after.

Q. What did Mr. O'Connell say after that?

A. Mr. O'Connell said he would never give him immunity in the Chillingworth case.

Q. Did you have any conversation with Joe Peel after that?

A. Yes.

Q. Where?

A. I followed him to an adjacent office . . . Soon after Joe Peel entered, I said: "Joe, if you say you had nothing to do with it, will you please tell me why you want immunity?" He pointed his finger at me and said: "Henry, I've got to have immunity. I've got to have it."

In cross-examining Lovern, the gentlemanly Mr. Welch began to show bitterness. He felt that he was fighting the state of Florida—and sometimes his client—alone. Welch stood and mimicked Lovern saying: "I've got to have immunity. I've got to have immunity." He asked Agent Lovern if he took shorthand notes and, if not, how he could remember the dialogue so precisely. He did not, however, shake Lovern's testimony, and the state now had corroboration that Judge Peel had asked for immunity in the Chillingworth murder case, and had been turned down.

The only smile of the day occurred when Jukin' George Thomas, a Negro bolita operator, took the stand to testify that Judge Peel had offered him protection from raids and arrests for $50 a week. Jukin' George was a sad man. The protection did him little good. He left the stand wearing a uniform of prison denim. He is finishing a five-year term.

FIFTEENTH
DAY

The Palm Beach murder case closed on a whimper today. Some prominent citizens of Palm Beach took the witness stand to say, in monotonous chorus, that they knew Joseph A. Peel and that his reputation was bad. A few others, including Peel's former secretary, took random shots at him as he sat drumming his fingers on the council table. Once or twice, he muttered: "God damn you! You son of a bitch!" His onetime law associate, Harold Gray, said that Peel had introduced him to Floyd Holzapfel and had described Lucky as an "awning salesman."

Mr. Carlton Welch made two motions for a mistrial. Both were denied. One witness, a laconic filling-station operator, testified that he had bought $10,000 worth of stock in Insured

182

Capital Corporation. All he got back was $66 interest. The final witness was a jailer from Palm Beach who testified that Judge Peel's brother John was in the habit of bringing Winston cigarettes to Joe, but no one bothered to examine them for poison.

Before noon, a witness said "I don't know" to a final question, and the matter of the State of Florida *versus* Joseph A. Peel came to a close. Judge Smith called counsel to the bench and there was a whispered conference as the spectators got up, yawning and snapping their galluses, and left.

The judge got the attention of the jury and said: "Gentlemen of the jury: counsel for the state and for the defense, together with the court, appreciates very much the patience that you have shown. There are matters which must be handled between the attorneys, both for the state and for the defense, and the court, out of your presence.

"Something other than a few minutes time will be required in order to appropriately handle the matter. You may rest assured that counsel for the state and for the defense, together with the court, will handle them as expeditiously as possible. As stated last night and before, the court is sure you realize that the admonitions to you by the court and the repeating of them is not given to you to bore you, they are given to you because of their importance and that you may ever have them uppermost in your minds, and that, having them in your minds, you will adhere strictly to them."

The jury was dismissed. Judge Smith asked counsel to confer with him in chambers at 2 P.M. At that time, he wanted them to suggest instructions which he might include in his charge to the jury. After the conference, he said, the matter would be recessed until the morning.

Both sides agreed to limit summations to four hours for each

183

side. The state would open the final argument; the defense would then be given four hours time, and the state would close the summations. Judge Smith asked what time court should convene in the morning. "Gentlemen, is it to be nine or nine-thirty?"

Phil O'Connell put on a mock hangdog expression. "Nine, your honor," he said. "Gonna be a lot of hot air tomorrow and we need time."

SIXTEENTH DAY

The morning was clear and hot. In court, the air conditioner thumped like the heart of a great beast who could live and die at will. Judge Smith swept in promptly at nine, a gracious forbearing jurist who had won the respect of the press. The bailiff rapped for order. The attorneys stopped drawing sheets of foolscap from their briefcases. The spectators stood. Sheriff Jack Norvel, badge on jacket lapel, walked up to the bench and whispered to the judge.

The judge looked puzzled. He called Assistant Defense Counsel Jack Rogers of Fort Pierce to him. There was a whispered conference. A bailiff hurried out the corridor and came back shaking his head. It was the day of final summation, and no one

185

could find Mr. Carlton Welch. Peel heard the news, and grinned. O'Connell bowed curtly to Judge Smith and said that the state was ready.

Mr. Welch, it seemed, had an unconscious disrespect for time. He had become mired in irrelevancies on many occasions in this trial and on others he had had little control of witnesses, or even their time of arrival. It was agreed yesterday that court would convene at nine. At 9:10, Mr. Jack Rogers was on the telephone in the hall outside trying to locate Welch. The judge left the bench, went back to his chambers, and waited. Rogers said that Welch was on his way.

At 9:30, the chief of defense counsel arrived. He seemed surprised to find everyone in court, waiting. He consulted his watch and said that he had understood . . . Judge Smith said his apology was accepted, and to please start the proceedings. The jury was called in. Welch's attention was drawn, every few minutes, by Peel, who whispered of legal points he wanted mentioned. Welch appeared to be slightly irritated with the defendant, and on a few occasions when Peel called him, the lawyer pretended he did not hear.

Assistant State Attorney Charles F. Brown led off for the prosecution. In all, there were four summations, two by each side. The next day, Judge Smith would charge the jury. It has always been a source of wonder that any jury, no matter how discerning, can manage to listen to hundreds of thousands of words of testimony, separating the essential from the nonessential, the credible from the incredible and then, at the conclusion, sit through the windy special pleadings of counsel, and the dusty legalistic oratory of the judge, and try to arrive at a just verdict.

"May it please the court," said Mr. Brown, "gentlemen of the jury, I would like again to say good morning. I know all of you are just as happy as we are that we have reached this stage of the trial. As you know all that has been said during the course of this trial for three weeks, we are now at that point where counsel will argue and the court will present its charge."

Many years ago, lawyers found that it pays to pander to juries, either apologizing for the length of the trial, complimenting them for their intelligence and fortitude, or moving the mundane business of murder into the realm of patriotism. Brown decided to try them all.

"This has been a useful trial in many respects," he said. "You gentlemen have been here for many weeks away from your homes, and your businesses and your families. That certainly has been a hardship on you. I think when you reflect why you are here, you will realize that it has been a hardship, but you gentlemen represent the very foundation on which this government of ours is built. You are a jury to try a criminal case. Under our system of government, every man under a criminal charge is entitled to be tried by a jury. That is the only way it should be. We are one of the very few countries left to be able to do it this way. We know that you have made sacrifices.

"I am sure that when you have concluded your deliberation and are discharged, you can walk from this courtroom proud of the fact that you have brought a service to your county, state and nation. Likewise, your families. I would like to say too that of all the trials which I have had anything to do with, I have never had a jury which was as attentive to the testimony, instructions by the court, and arguments of the counsel as you gentlemen were. I am sure everyone in this courtroom joins me in that announcement. You have shown attentiveness, patience in this case. That is the way it should be."

Having buttered the boys to the brows, Brown buttressed

187

the recollections of the jurors by reciting the stories of the state's witnesses in brief, starting with the discovery that the Chillingworths were missing from their Manalapan home on June 15, 1955. It was a now-we-come-to summation with, here and there, a shot at Joe Peel. Mr. Brown said that the only similarity between Chillingworth and Peel was that both were judges.

The jurors paid no more attention than they had throughout the trial. Some stared at the stained ceiling; some stared at the speaker as though looking at him but thinking of something else; some appeared to absorb every word; a few looked chronically puzzled.

Brown recited the evidence against Peel succinctly and ably, and closed by pointing out that "Justice is not a one-way street down which this man, or any other defendant, can walk unimpeded by law and order and respect for the rights of others."

When he concluded, there was a short recess. Then Assistant Defense Attorney Jack Rogers, a soft-voiced southerner, opened for Joe Peel. His chore was difficult because the weighty part of the evidence was with the prosecution. Rogers, a dark man with a mustache, decided to stick to definitions of law for his opening. His sole function, and that of Carlton Welch, was to create a doubt in the minds of the jurors.

In one sentence he dispensed with thanking the jury for its valiance in sitting on its hips for three weeks. Then he moved on to the matter of witnesses, and advised the jury that the manner of witnesses, as they testify, is important. So too is bias or prejudice on the part of a witness; his interest in the outcome of the trial; his credibility; even his intelligence.

Rogers remained near the bench, talking to the jury from a distance of eight or ten feet. His voice was drawling, dispassionate; he sounded like a professor reciting an old lesson to a new class.

"Gentlemen, you can only find Joe Peel guilty of these charges," he said. "This is the only thing Joe Peel is on trial for. Whether or not he might have been connected with any other alleged act has no bearing. It is for you to determine whether he is correctly charged as an accessory before the fact of the death of C. E. Chillingworth. In determining this cause, it must be proved beyond and to the exclusion of every reasonable doubt. You are reasonable men and that is the same reasonable doubt that we are concerned with here. Reasonable doubt . . .

"Now then, the state has also stated that Mr. Peel was afraid of the Shupe case. That Judge Chillingworth would get him because of the Shupe case. After being before him once on this, then the most Peel could look for was suspension or possible disbarment.

"But I would like to call your attention to one of the state's witnesses, Mrs. McEwan, the judge's secretary. She came to this stand and testified to some extent about the extended vacation that Judge Chillingworth was getting ready to take in Europe. Now, how would the death of C. E. Chillingworth help this man if there was a possibility that these charges would be brought while the judge was in Europe? There was another judge, Judge White, who testified that in the absence of Judge Chillingworth a judge from Fort Lauderdale would have come up and heard it. So why, why would the death of Judge Chillingworth in the Shupe case benefit Judge Peel?"

Rogers then moved on to fan the natural prejudices of the southern jury. Bobby Lincoln was a Negro. He was a self-confessed party to the murder of a white judge. Floyd Holzapfel was a notorious and callous criminal. Why grant immunity to the Negro to get the judge? Why accept a plea of guilty from Lucky, and then postpone sentence pending his appearance as a state witness against the judge? The feeling all over Florida was that Phil O'Connell was determined to put Peel in the electric chair no matter how high the price in prejudice.

"They are suspicious of three people," Rogers said. "What do they do? Give Bobby Lincoln, confessed murderer of three murders by his own testimony, immunity. They took a hardened criminal, one who admitted he fired a bullet into a man lying on the ground and tied up. They didn't explain to you why Holzapfel did not receive his opportunity to be sentenced. They were waiting for this trial. He hasn't been sentenced to this day. Will he get the electric chair? Or will he get off with a lighter sentence?"

The lawyer decided to dispense with Joe Peel's testimony briefly. "I want you to recall Joe Peel's testimony. He looked you in the eye. He didn't hide one thing. Not one thing. Every question that was asked of him, he answered. He was not shaken in his testimony."

Always, always, the defense had to return to a doubt. Cite one, create one, devise one. "What if it is found out at a later date that Judge Chillingworth did not die as alleged in the indictment, but that the body was found in a shallow grave some place—or not at all?"

The day moved on, and when the spectators found out what summation means, they began to tiptoe out of the room. There was little that could be called electrifying in what the lawyers were saying. In fact, the monologues were, at best, gracious gestures permitting assistant counsel to star, for an hour or so, in a drama in which the state of Florida was trying to prove that it is so wrong to take a life that another one must be taken as a penalty so that others will not commit the same wrong.

Before noon, Mr. Eugene Spellman got his chance. Mr. Spellman was a lawyer's lawyer. In a profession noted for oral circumlocution, this little man was a potential giant. He did not drop his g's and use cracker slang to impress the jury, nor did he use dramatics to draw his points. At the start of his argument, Spellman told the story of the case in one long paragraph:

"The court will instruct you that there are four elements that the state must prove beyond and exclusive of any reasonable doubt. The state first must prove the death of C. E. Chillingworth. The state must, second, prove that he died of a criminal agency. The state must prove, third, that Judge Chillingworth was murdered by drowning by Floyd A. Holzapfel and we must prove, fourth, that Joseph Alexander Peel, Jr., counseled, hired, persuaded and commanded said Floyd A. Holzapfel to kill Judge Chillingworth."

He then expounded on these things point by point. In the first, Spellman cleverly braided two items of contention. One was how to prove that there was a murder when there was no corpus delicti. The second was why grant immunity to Lincoln.

"You will hear a great deal of the word why. Why, the defense will ask, did they give that big, mean, murdering black boy immunity? Why didn't we prosecute him along with Holzapfel and along with Peel? For the simple reason, gentlemen, that we have got to prove the death of C. E. Chillingworth. We have to have direct evidence to present to this jury.

"We could not bring back the body, so we had to give one of the three immunity from prosecution, so that he could come on this stand as a witness and give direct evidence about the viciousness and heinousness of this crime. You might say—why Lincoln? Why not Holzapfel? Why not Peel?

"Peel denies it, but I don't think there is any question—according to the testimony of Sidney Catts, Henry Lovern and

Ross Anderson—that this man was the first to come and ask for immunity from the prosecutor in this case. 'I will tell you the facts if you will give me immunity.' We gave Bobby Lincoln immunity because, of the three men, he is the most insignificant. He was an employee of Floyd Holzapfel . . .

"Gentlemen, let me ask you this. Let me ask each and every one of you this question as if we were not in a trial and I came to you with our problem: we cannot present a body. We need direct evidence to conclude the case. If I came to you, would you say don't give any of them immunity, let them all go free, or would you say give the least participant immunity so that you can put the other two in the electric chair where they belong?

"I say to you that it is unfortunate that Bobby Lincoln was given immunity. He should be treated as we hope the other two will be. Floyd Holzapfel signed his death warrant when he took this stand. I submit that this man who sits in this courtroom today, Joseph Alexander Peel, Jr., deserves no less."

Late in the afternoon, Carlton Welch stood to make his address. He sipped water from a paper cup, and as he began to speak, he walked back and forth across the front of the jury box, looking up, looking down, talking in the almost abstract manner of a man talking to himself. He had lost so much weight in the past three weeks that he looked like a shaved Lincoln, the profile on a worn penny.

"I have been frightened," he said slowly, deliberately, sincerely, "for the last six, eight, twelve weeks. I have been frightened. I would not be telling you an untruth. The fact that a human life rests in my hands is not what I'm frightened about. I'm frightened because the state, in a capital offense, has attempted to evade the burden of proof and to shift the burden on the defendant."

192

The attack was nebulous. It shifted swiftly in a you-all stream of consciousness, as though it weren't necessary to explain the points of the summation to the jury. Sometimes Welch paused to take a long, silent look at Judge D. C. Smith, who was working on his charge to the jury with pencil and long sheets of yellow paper.

"Joe Peel was a lawyer. He wasn't very good, I'm sorry to say, because he did not keep up with the local rules of the bar association." He talked for a while about an invasion of the courtroom akin to one in Cuba, except that Welch's hypothetical invasion was a matter of poisonous propaganda. Monotonously, he kept repeating "that brings us to the point," but he didn't get to the point for two hours.

He quoted five proverbs from Solomon in the Book of Proverbs, and he quoted Shakespeare to define the word "equivocation." Macbeth, by some weird stretch of southern chivalry, became a "cotton pickin' character." At one point, he reached for the package of cigarettes which the state contended held cyanide of potassium intended for Lucky Holzapfel's dinner. He was waving it before the jury as Mrs. Peel entered the courtroom carrying a package of cigarettes for her husband.

"Do you want to examine these?" said Mrs. Peel to Sheriff Norvel. He bowed gallantly. "No, ma'am. You take 'em right on in."

He attacked all who opposed his client. Henry Lovern was a man with "photographic ears. He has the power to repeat verbatim a conversation between two men five months ago. Such a performance is unknown to science." There was no doubt, he told the jury, about which way Ross Anderson's sympathies lay in this case. These men were out to get Peel, to entrap him.

If anyone questioned Peel's honesty, all he would have to do was to recall the testimony that Joe phoned Lawyer Catts to ask, in good conscience, if he could "release information about Holzapfel's participation in the Harvey killing." Peel was, Mr. Welch maintained, the epitome of the good citizen. He cited the $10,000 check given by the filling-station man to invest in Insured Capital Corporation. It was endorsed, the lawyer said, by Insured Capital.

"If Joe Peel was as crooked as the state would like to have you believe, he could have cashed that check and been $10,000 richer."

Peel's only fear, it seemed, was Floyd Holzapfel. The fear grew and grew and became unreasonable. "Holzapfel understood this, and that's why he made a threat to Johnny Peel, that if he was picked up for the Harvey case he would turn state's evidence against Peel in the Chillingworth case."

When the prosecution had Bobby Lincoln delivered from the federal prison, it didn't have time to coach him in his testimony, and that was why, Welch said, Lincoln gave details of the Chillingworth murder which were at variance with those told by Lucky.

Sometimes, it appeared, Mr. Welch had lapses of his own. Speaking of the porch light on the Chillingworth home, he said: "That light was a signal for Bobby Lincoln, who was waiting in a car on the road, to go into action. He dragged the judge out of his house and placed his body on the floor of the car. Three men drove away from the house shortly after eleven o'clock that night, as one witness here testified."

The witness did not testify that Bobby Lincoln was in a car, or that three men drove away from the Chillingworth home. He said he saw a car about that time of night southbound on Route

194

1A1 from the direction of the Chillingworth home. Then, too, if Chillingworth was on the floor of the car, what happened to Mrs. Chillingworth?

"Gentlemen, you can only go to the electric chair once, for one murder or for three murders. Does guilt by association go in this country? We are in America. Or are we?"

He deplored the evidence about events in Orlando, Eau Gallie and Melbourne. They diverted the attention of the jury from the Chillingworth case, Welch maintained. "This is all part of a plot for Floyd Holzapfel to seek revenge on this boy and take him to the electric chair with him."

He shook his head sadly. "They tried to bring Peel's wife into this. They tried to bring his brother into it. They have tried to blacken the Peel name. They want you to base your verdict on passion and prejudice and anxiety and fear. They have pointed out that the way to gain the favor of the ruler is to do something against Joe Peel."

If, said Mr. Welch, looking at the jury with his long fingers out front in an attitude of supplication, if the state attorney wanted to solve the matter, "he could have called Peel in on a subpoena instanter and said: 'You're going to tell us something about the Chillingworth case or plead the Fifth Amendment.' Then we might have had something."

What it is that the state of Florida might have had, Welch did not say. At the conclusion of his talk, the defense attorney said: "I stand here before you with no intention that is not your intention, no purpose that is not your purpose. Use your common sense and judgment." Under his breath, the lawyer said: "May you see the right as God gives you to see the right. God bless you."

Judge Peel watched the performance closely. His elbows were

on the counsel table, his lips were on his knuckles. He was using three expressions: contrition, which was achieved with lowered lashes and eyes on the table; geniality, which was done with flashing eyes and a rich smile; and anger, which was accompanied by a tight compression of the lips and a jabbing motion of the index finger.

Long before Mr. Welch had concluded, Judge Smith had finished taking notes and leaned back in his high-backed chair to close his eyes. Hershell Carlile, juror number two, studied his hands and began to move his eyes across the rows of spectators slowly. So did Elmer Hansen, the juror who forgot to bring his upper plate.

It was evening before Phillip O'Connell moved before the jurors. The state attorney was cast in the mold of the old-time trial lawyers who roar and whisper, beseech and demand, entreat and joke. He required an hour to say what he had to say. He was able and forceful, dominating and domineering.

There was a fat moon over the St. Lucie courthouse and the air was scented with night jasmine as O'Connell got to his feet to bury his old friend.

"I have lived since June fifteenth, 1955, for this hour," he said. The courtroom was again jammed. The townfolk were in attendance to hear personal venom, to be in on the kill. "The ghost of Judge Chillingworth walks tonight.

"He gave this man a chance." The prosecutor pointed over his back at the defendant. "Don't you think he knew what was going to happen to him when he faced Chillingworth the second time? He knew. What did he tell Wilder? He said 'Cold chills run up and down my back.' He knew."

There was a table in front of the jury box. O'Connell put one hip on it and folded his arms. "Smart fella," he said. "Clever.

But he walked in error. 'There is honor among thieves,' they say. They ain't no such thing. They huntin' for each other all the time. Who was the first one who wanted to tell on the others?" O'Connell pointed over his back at Peel.

The state attorney was a one-time fighter, a man with a chronic competitive instinct. "Peel requested to see me," he said. "But he ain't that good a salesman. Did he have enough reason to kill Judge Chillingworth? If we knew how much is enough we might be able to stop crime. His lawyer says: 'Would a reasonable man do this?' I don't think Joe Peel is a reasonable man. He has the most warped mind I have ever known. Who corrupted who? Did Holzapfel corrupt Peel, who corrupted Bobby Lincoln? What does it matter? As far as the state is concerned, Holzapfel signed his own death warrant right here, right on this witness stand."

Then, softly: "But this one was the brains. The leader. No matter how much you think you know, you can't make a move until one of them is ready to talk. Peel was the first who wanted to talk. We turned him down.

"Peel made Bobby Lincoln the biggest nigger in West Palm Beach. He walked big. He could say 'I got the judge in my hand' and he could prove it by saying 'Get your warrant and raid 410 Rosemary Street and I'll get a phone call before you get here.'

"Before that, Lincoln was never convicted of a crime. Who made him a murderer? P. O. Wilber was never, until that time, convicted of a crime. Jim Yenzer was never convicted of a crime."

The prosecutor ridiculed a defense contention that Peel could not inform on Lucky and Bobby because of his oath as a lawyer. "He had been out of the practice of law eight months be-

197

fore," O'Connell said. "Who do you think whispered in Lincoln's ear and made him a murderer? That fellow right there."

Speaking of Judge Peel, O'Connell said: "He came here with a pat story of half-truths and he denied what he could. He was the most intelligent witness on the stand. It makes me sick to hear him talk about his honesty."

He said that the reason why Peel wanted immunity, and was in such a hurry to get it, was because he believed that Jim Yenzer had just killed Floyd Holzapfel. That would leave Peel and the Negro as the two remaining plotters in the Chillingworth murder.

"If this had happened, "O'Connell shouted, "Peel was home free. I believe that Joe Peel must forfeit his life to the state of Florida and I ask you for a verdict of guilty with no mercy."

It was a strong plea, an able plea, a personal plea. No one could doubt that, as a matter of law, Mr. O'Connell had presented a solid case for the state of Florida from the opening of the trial until now. As court recessed, and the reporters walked out of the court into the night, someone took a poll. It was eleven to one that the jury would send Judge Peel to the electric chair.

SEVENTEENTH
DAY

We sat in the detention room in the jail. Judge Peel had sent
word that he would like to have breakfast with me on the big
day. It was cool as I walked down to the back of the St. Lucie
County prison; a fresh breeze out of the southeast stirred
thousands of white feathers on the bosom of the Indian River.

The young judge was waiting. There was a long table and a
couple of chairs in the detention room on the ground floor and
a high window with steel mesh outside. He was knotting a brown
tie. He stood and flashed his big smile and held out his hand.
He had nerve, up to a point.

We talked about the judge's charge to the jury, which would
begin in thirty minutes. By noon, perhaps earlier, the jury would
be out to deliberate a verdict. Everything—bad and good—

which had happened before was leading directly to this day. The tension did not seem to touch Joe Peel. He finished tying the knot, and pulled the tie up to the collar.

I asked him what he thought would happen. "I think I'll get a hung jury," he said. He thought for a moment or two and said: "Maybe a not guilty, but a hung jury for sure."

It isn't easy to read the heart of a man, but I have never known an innocent man who didn't insist that he was about to be acquitted. Sometimes even those who were guilty and felt guilty talked of acquittal. This man was the first to talk of a hung jury.

"What do you think?" he said.

I was sorry he asked. "It may be pretty bad," I said lamely. "It could be pretty bad."

Outside, we could hear feminine heels on the concrete walk. Judge Peel began to grin again. "I know that walk," he said in singsong happiness. Outside, a woman's voice said: "Jo—seph!" It was Mrs. Peel. She went to the back door, said good morning to the deputies around the radio desk, and came to the detention room. In her hand was a Thermos of coffee. Behind her was a middle-aged man. This was Imogene's father, Mr. A. B. Clark of Lake City, Florida.

Mrs. Peel wore a green and white silk skirt and a white blouse. She too radiated confidence. The Peels wore smiles as part of the ensemble of the day. I had seen each of them when the smiles were down. On those occasions, both of them presented expressions which were puffy and morose.

The young judge had higher emotional peaks, and deeper valleys, than Imogene. Sometimes a small bit of good news would cause him to climb toward ecstasy and he would clap his hands like a child. At other times, he would drop suddenly to the bottomless pit of despair, staring at the floor, the eyes wide and unblinking, the mouth open. When he first got to this jail, the guards found him one night sliding off his bunk. Peel had swallowed a fistful of sleeping pills.

He offered some coffee. I declined. We talked about the trial. He wasn't pleased with it. "I was let down in many instances," he said. "I was frustrated for days on end. There were differences of opinion between Carl and me." His father-in-law shook his head sympathetically.

"There were differences in tactics too," Judge Peel said. "Some people said I masterminded my own trial. It's untrue. In every instance, I acceded to Carl. When we differed, he won."

I asked him what he proposed to do with his life if he were acquitted. He looked up at the slices of lemon sun coming through the barred window. "There are so many cases against me," he said. "I don't think I'll go free. Phil is committed to prosecute me." Among the charges which the judge would have to face were (1) Mrs. Chillingworth's murder; (2) plot to kill Floyd Holzapfel; (3) about 160 counts of fraud in connection with Insured Capital Corporation.

If he was found guilty, would he appeal? "Oh, yes," he said quickly. "Oh, yes. Right through the state courts up to the Supreme Court of the United States, if necessary. Oh, yes."

Had he, as a lawyer, seen any reversible error in this trial? "Uh-huh," the judge said. He ran his hand through his brown hair. "We listened to the tapes in chambers, as you know. Judge Smith wanted to hurry the process. We, the defense, wanted to listen to all of them. The judge called Henry Lovern in and he would say: 'Anything on this tape? Anything on that one?'

"If Lovern said no, we didn't get to hear it. Lovern is with the prosecution. He was a witness against me. Is it fair for the judge to ask Lovern what is worth listening to? I think we can get a new trial on that mistake."

I knew that he and Phil O'Connell had once been friends. I wanted to know how friendly.

"In March 1951," he said, "I was appointed City Prosecutor in West Palm Beach. I was a kid, two years out of law school. Phil, of course, was state attorney. He was a big man and he had a big law practice. He asked me if I would like to come into his office and work with him. I agreed. He paid the office rent. I paid my own secretary.

"Phil put me on as associate counsel with him on many cases. My reception room was Phil's reception room. We didn't socialize much, but I went to a few cocktail parties at his home. Sometimes we met at dances. Yes, Phil was once my friend."

What would he change if he could start all over again?

"I would not enter politics, for one thing. Not at all. I would not enter the practice of criminal law either. I'd go into civil law. With a civil law practice, I would not get to meet men like Floyd Holzapfel and Bobby Lincoln. These were mistakes. Bad mistakes.

"I sit and think about them. I have time to think of lots of things. When I was suspended from the practice of law, I should never have returned to Palm Beach. I should have stayed away. Even in this trial, I have made mistakes.

"Several times, I wanted to run up to Judge Smith and say: 'I'm not getting a fair trial. Help me.' I knew after the second day that Carl was not equal to this job. Instead of doing something about it, getting another lawyer or asking the court to appoint one, I sat and wrung my hands."

A deputy stuck his head in the door and said it was time to

go to court. I shook hands with the young judge, and wished him luck. The big smile was turned on again, and Mrs. Peel said she'd see me in court.

The courtroom was half full. The people of Fort Pierce sensed that there would be no excitement in Judge Smith's charge, that he would adhere to the desiccated points of law, and that the jury would listen, half aware of the many admonitions to be fair, and then retire to take God knows how long to arrive at a verdict.

Peel was brought in grinning. He nodded to his counsel and waved hello to some Palm Beach newspapermen, who sat with notebooks on crossed knees. The newspapermen had been guessing, among themselves, whether it would require a lot of time for the jury to reach a verdict. The guesses were varied, but one Florida sage said that no jury, at a time like this, was going to waste time in deliberation. "Those men will get in there, take a poll, find out which way the majority is thinking, and then all will fall in line. We'll have a verdict before supper."

The bailiff rapped for order, and Judge Smith began his charge. He read from notes and required twenty-three minutes to complete it. The speech was a marvel of umpirical fairness. It was so free of bias as to be almost antiseptic. He concluded by saying:

"Your verdict must be the verdict of each and every juror, each juror being responsible for his own verdict, and any verdict as to the defendant's guilt or innocence must be unanimous, that is, it must be concurred in by each of you. Whatever verdict you find must be signed by one of your members as foreman, and when you retire to the consideration of your verdict you should elect one of your number to serve in the capacity of foreman.

"You may retire, gentlemen, to the consideration of your verdict."

Before the jury left, the judge excused the two alternates, a retired police lieutenant from Washington, D.C., and a retired shop owner. They asked permission to sit outside the rail and await the verdict. It was granted. When the jury departed to the big room behind the court, the judge said he had a special word to say to the press, and would everyone please remain seated.

Smith, wearing a solemn, judicial expression, said he wanted to thank the reporters one and all for their fairness, not only in abiding by the rules laid down by the court, but for their coverage of the trial itself. "For this," he said with no smile, "I'm giving all of you an A-plus." As an afterthought, he said: "If any of you ever need a letter to your editor, see me." The courtroom broke into laughter and the judge joined it.

The long wait began. The court emptied and Joe Peel sat alone chatting with Mrs. Peel. The spectators stood close to the rail, watching the man whose life now hung on the minute hand of the clock. Judge Smith went to his chambers, and sent a bailiff out for a reporter.

"It's a hot day," the judge said. "I know it's the practice of you fellows to leave one of your number in court in case the jury comes in. I want to make a suggestion. You fellows go wherever you propose to go, and leave your phone number with me. When the jury is ready to come in, I'll be notified and I'll call you. Then I'll take a little time in chambers—say ten minutes. That should give you all enough time to get in court for the verdict. Is that satisfactory?"

It couldn't be better. The reporter left the phone number of the pressroom around the corner, and thanked the judge. Then everyone left to file early stories. After that the clock slowed. The minutes ticked by and people stood on the grass in front of the old courthouse to look up at the big bay window where the jury deliberated.

The sun inched higher, and Peel asked to be taken back to his cell. O'Connell and Eugene Spellman left a phone number with the bailiff and went back to the Southernaire Motel, where there was air conditioning and a swimming pool. Inside the prison it was quiet. All the tenants knew that this was a big day, an if day, a perhaps day, for one of their number. On most other days, sporadic singing could be heard through the screens and bars. But not today.

In the late morning, a bailiff heard a knocking on the jury door and he ran and summoned the judge, the sheriff and all interested parties. Men ran through the corridors yelling, "Verdict. Verdict. Jury coming in." The judge phoned the reporters, who left their typewriters and trotted the block and a half to the court.

When everyone had assembled, the judge said: "Let the jury be brought in." They came in, mostly in shirtsleeves, and their faces showed nothing. One of them, Mr. Ruhl L. Day, announced that he had been elected foreman and would speak for the others. He said that the jury had not arrived at a verdict, but would like to ask for some testimony to read.

The judge asked what testimony, and Mr. Ruhl said that one man wanted to read some of Holzapfel's statements, and others wanted to reread some of Wilber's. One man wanted to listen to the tapes. The judge called a conference of counsel at the bench—a whispering *voir dire*—and agreed that it would be impossible to comply with the wishes of the jury. None of the testimony had been transcribed from shorthand to typewritten words. The tapes could not be played because much of it had not been admitted as evidence and would require positive identification of several voices.

The request was denied. The judge said that, while the jury was present, he would permit them to go to lunch under guard, and that they could resume their deliberations at 1:30 P.M. It was a false alarm, and the court emptied slowly.

At 1:30 P.M. the reporters came back into court. Some sat and chatted. Some stood with spectators in the hall, smoking. The full heat of the day oppressed the city and there was little traffic, except the big trailer trucks en route south to Miami, 120 miles away, or north to New York, 1,350 miles away. There was a big white thunderhead in the western sky and an old farmer squinted at it and said: "Might rain before the day is over."

At 2 P.M. the court was quiet again. The sheriff sat alone inside the enclosure, his hands folded across his chest. In the jury box an old bailiff sat with his feet up on the railing, reading. Downstairs someone put dimes in the coke machine. A clerk tacked public notices on the front door.

At 3 o'clock the jury sent out word that it would like to know whether Peel had used the Fifth Amendment when asked about his conversations with Yenzer regarding the "C" case. Judge Smith told them that, to ascertain such a matter, they would have to hear the testimony of several witnesses all over again. He told them to return to their deliberations and think about it. If they wanted to hear the pertinent testimony again, they should send word to him.

Apparently the men decided to drop it. The clock slowed again and the minutes dragged their feet. Peel told a jailer that the longer the jury took to reach a verdict, the better it looked for him. Most of the lawyers standing around the halls agreed that there was no room for a mercy verdict. It would be guilty or not guilty. If the jury believed that Judge Peel devised the murders, then it would have to believe that it was done with premeditation and malice and careful planning.

It could not be classified as a crime of passion, which is sometimes partially excusable. If the jury believed that Peel was not a party to the Chillingworth murders, then they should acquit him at once because, in that event, none of the state's case was worth consideration. The lawyers seemed to feel that, on the evidence, Peel would be sentenced to the electric chair.

At 4 P.M. the local radio stations were issuing bulletins on the case, and some of the citizens left their homes to come to court. The seats were crowded again and the bailiffs were busy telling women not to talk loudly, and not to smoke.

The waiting continued. The judge was in his chambers, talking to visiting jurists who had stopped by to hear a verdict. Outside, the sky was darkening and a few men rushed down to the parking lot to put the tops up on their cars. At 4:30 P.M. there was a loud clap of thunder and a long roll of drums walking off into the distance; at the same time, a knock was heard on the jury door.

The old bailiff reading in the jury box sprang to his feet, opened the door a crack, listened, nodded, closed the door, and ran across the courtroom to Sheriff Norvel. They whispered, then Norvel and the bailiff hurried off in separate directions— Norvel to bring the prisoner in from the jail, the bailiff to notify Judge Smith that the jury had reached a verdict.

Norvel ordered a couple of deputies into action. They phoned the prosecution staff that the jury was ready with a verdict; they phoned the defense; the reporters received a call. The As-

207

sociated Press and United Press International sent similar flashes over the wires across the country:

FORT PIERCE, FLA.—PEEL JURY COMING IN WITH A VERDICT AT 4:30 P.M. MORE LATER.

In ten minutes the entire cast of characters of the trial had reassembled, for the last time, with each person in his appointed place. Joe Peel sat at the counsel table, studying his knuckles and frowning. Mrs. Peel sat in the last row of the spectators' benches. Two male relatives of the Chillingworths sat in front. O'Connell stood behind the prosecution table, solemn and growling. Welch sat beside his client in silence.

The judge looked at O'Connell. "The prosecution is ready," the state attorney said. Smith looked at Welch. "The defense is ready." The judge said: "Bring the jury in."

The door was opened, and the twelve men filed in. The court was in silence, except for the claps of thunder outside and the beating of heavy rain on the courtroom windows. The jurymen stood.

"Have you arrived at a verdict?" Judge Smith said.

"We have," the foreman said.

"Hand the verdict to the stenographer."

It was done. The court stenographer took the sheet of paper to Clerk Roger Poitras, a young French Canadian. Mr. Poitras handed it up to Judge Smith. Smith read it carefully and handed it back to Poitras. Peel's eyes followed this procedure with the wistful expression of a hound dog watching a small bird flit from tree to tree.

The judge nodded to the clerk. "Read it," he said. Poitras glanced at the sheet, cleared his throat, and read:

"We the jury find Joseph Alexander Peel, Jr., guilty of being an accessory before the fact in the murder of C. E. Chillingworth and a majority of us recommend mercy."

208

Peel lifted his shoulders and then let them sag. Mrs. Peel burst into tears and rushed out of court with her father. An old man, who had dozed through most of the sessions as a spectator, looked across the aisle at me and murmured: "Is that all?"

Judge Smith polled each juror. "Is the verdict that was just read your verdict?" "Yes, your honor." So said they all.

Smith called Peel to the bench to advise him that he had been found guilty with a recommendation of mercy. "The court adjudges you guilty," said Smith. He set a date for sentencing, and the sentence was mandatory: life imprisonment.

The jury was thanked for its time and patience, and the men filed out to collect their warrants for $125 apiece. The judge called a conference in his chambers, and in a few minutes Mr. Welch came out, jingling coins in his trousers pocket.

"I will not appeal," he said. "I cannot afford it. I will be out, as Joe's lawyer, just as soon as the court will allow me." Jack Rogers, associate defense counsel, also left the conference. This implied that Joe Peel was inside, fighting for whatever was left to fight for, by himself. He had no counsel.

The verdict was no victory for O'Connell. He had started off with three murderers. To one he had granted immunity; the second pleaded guilty; the third had won mercy from a jury which admitted that it was in a hurry to get home for the holidays. The state attorney still had the murder of Mrs. Chillingworth to hold over Judge Peel's head, but he wasn't sure he wanted to go through all of this again.

When the judicial conference was over, Joe Peel came out saying "No comment" to all questions. If he felt bad, he didn't show it. In this trial he was the victor. He escaped with his life.

Someone asked Phil O'Connell what he thought of the verdict. "The ghost of Judge Chillingworth will never rest until his killers are shoveling coal in hell and the fires of damnation."

The young judge, flanked by deputies, left the courthouse and went down the wet walk to the jail. On his arm was Imogene Peel. She was saying: "There will be another day to fight." Her eyes were dry now. She was right. Her husband may serve between seven and ten years, and then be paroled.

The only man who brooded was Floyd Holzapfel. He found out that, after all his work in assisting the prosecution of Peel, the reward was a sentence of death in the electric chair.